ren

en fr

The Encyclopedia of
SMALL SPOT
ENGRAVINGS

A COPYRIGHT FREE HANDBOOK OF MATERIAL FOR REFERENCE OR REUSE
IN ADVERTISING OR PUBLICATIONS—WITHOUT PERMISSION OR PAYMENT

A COPYRIGHT FREE HANDBOOK COMPILED BY DICK SUTPHEN

COPYRIGHT 1969 BY
DICK SUTPHEN SCOTTSDALE, ARIZONA

MANUFACTURED IN USA—LIBRARY OF CONGRESS CARD NUMBER 72 89858
SBN PUBLISHERS NUMBER 911842   SBN LOG BOOK NUMBER 911842-00-4

CONTENTS

AMERICA

BATTLE BETWEEN THE "MONITOR" AND "MERRIMAC" IN HAMPTON ROADS.

A. Boston Battery.   B. Charlestown.   C. British Troops attacking.   D. Provincial Lines.

Bunker Hill Battle.

From a Contemporary Print, entitled "View of the Attack on Bunker's Hill, with the Burning of Charlestown, June 17th, 1775."

AN APPEAL TO HEAVEN

Pine Tree Flag.

Union Flag.

DONT TREAD ON ME

Rattlesnake Flag.

Boston Massacre. — From an Engraving by Paul Revere.

G. W. Maynard, Pinx.

1776.

J. Rae, Eng.

Columbia

THE LINCOLN MONUMENT—THE ARMY.

C. Conrad, Sc.   C Serz Eng.

THE AMERICAN SOLDIER

THE LINCOLN MONUMENT—THE NAVY.

Etruscan Canopic Vases.

Psykter in red-figured pottery: style of the artist Euthymides, 5th century, B. C.

Apulian Stamnos, in the Museo Nazionale, Naples.

Decorated Amphora from Ruvo, Italy.

Aiguière of silver gilt in the Pitti Palace, Florence.

Black-figured Bombylius.

Ancient Acerra.

Leaden Ampulla in the Museum at York, England. (From the "Journal of the British Archæological Association.")

Greek Vase, decorated in the Corinthian style.

Aftaba of copper with disks of white and blue enamel; Persian, 18th century.

Affixes. Italo-Greek Vase in the Campana Collection, Louvre Museum. (From "L'Art pour Tous.")

Censer, 13th century. (From Viollet-le-Duc's "Dict. du Mobilier français.")

Sofa with two Settees, 18th century.

Crater of Euphronios, Louvre Museum.— Greek red-figured pottery.

Biberon.— Oiron faïence (France), in South Kensington Museum, London. (From "L'Art pour Tous.")

A Shaped Mirror, 18th century.

Ancient Roman Cameo-Glass.— Amphora from Pompeii, Museo Nazionale, Naples.

Toby of English Pottery, 18th century.

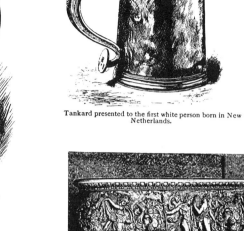

Tankard presented to the first white person born in New Netherlands.

Incised Bohemian Glass.—Museum of Fine Arts, Boston.

Agraffe—13th century.

The plate is in two parts; a hook behind the left-hand piece enters a ring behind the other. (From Viollet-le-Duc's "Dict. du Mobilier français.")

Bacchantes.—Mythological festival of Bacchus, from an ancient sarcophagus in the Vatican Museum.

Buhl.—Commode executed by Boule, in the Bibliothèque Mazarine, Paris. (From "L'Art pour Tous.")

Example of Modern Venetian Glass, with spray of flowers in color on a transparent body.

Fire-screen, covered with tapestry.—Louis-Seize style.

Specimens of Ancient Roman Glass.
(From "L'Art pour Tous.")

Fire-place in 16th Century.

Ear-rings:
Egyptian Government.

— KNOCKER — (15th century.)

Wreath or Brooch. Italian.

Chalice: late Renaissance (Virgile Solis).

Alms-basin decorated with champlevé enamel, 13th century.

Corporation Insignia, Record Book, and Loving Cup, Wenlock.

Cup: German, 1620.

SIDE OF A STONE SARCOPHAGUS FROM AMATHUS.

TERRA-COTTA VASE FOUND IN
A TOMB AT AMATHUS.

END OF A STONE SARCOPHAGUS.

TERRA-COTTA VASE.
FROM DALI.

Greek Lamp.

Kylix. (From an example in the Museum of Fine Arts, Boston.)

PRESENTOIR.

RING WITH EGYPTIAN DESIGN.

RING WITH CUPIDS.

SILVER OBJECT.

EGYPTIAN SCARABÆUS
WITH SILVER SWIVEL.

Pendant. Niello Work.

Faïence of Gien et Loiret: French Collective Exhibit.

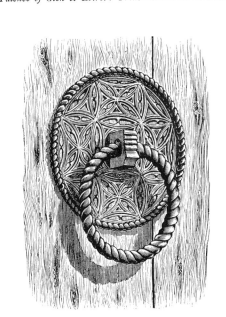

Door Handle (probably Flemish).

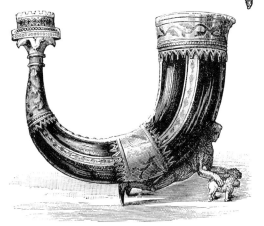

Louis XVI. Clock.

Mounted Horn: Pitti Palace.

Silver Scent-Bottle.

Flagon : German. Sixteenth Century.

Examples of Murano (Venetian) Glass, 16th century. (From "L'Art pour Tous.")

Vases: Daniell & Sons, London. From the collection of Sir Richard Wallace.

HUNTING CUP.

Beer - mug. — German pottery with pewter mountings; 18th century.

Onyx Vase.   Thomas Webb and Sons, Stourbridge.

Timepiece : Silver Gilt.   French (?) Renaissance.

Attic Lecythi.

Termination of
Dagger-sheath : Venetian.

Endicott's Sun Dial and other Colonial Relics.

Spinning Wheel.

Colonial Relics.

Bronze Inkstand.   Sixteenth Century.

Door Handle (English).

Candelabrum.

Mace and Tankard, Chesterfield.

TRIPOD.

Time Globe: L. P. Juvet, Glen's Falls, N. Y.

Mounted Horn: Pitti Palace.

Handle of Mirror

Pendant. German.

Pendant. German.

TERRA-COTTA HEADS—FROM TEMPLE OF APOLLO HYLATES.

Knocker (Mediæval).

ROMAN LAMPS.

CRADLE OF HENRY V.

Sampler

Kalpis.—Examples of Greek red-figured pottery.

Hand-Mirror.   French : Sixteenth Century.

Cameos : Starr & Marcus, New York.

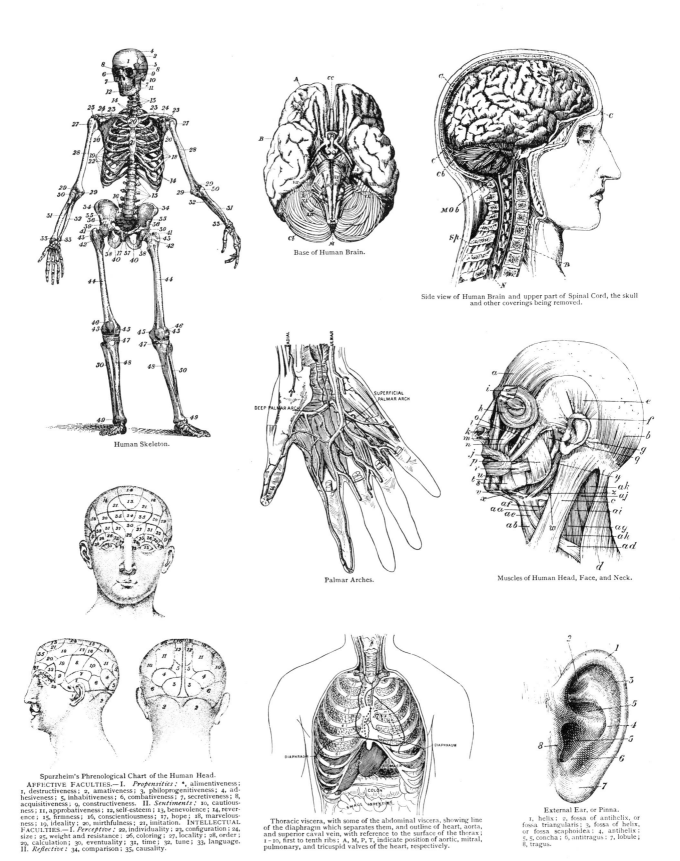

Human Skeleton.

Base of Human Brain.

Side view of Human Brain and upper part of Spinal Cord, the skull and other coverings being removed.

Palmar Arches.

Muscles of Human Head, Face, and Neck.

Spurzheim's Phrenological Chart of the Human Head.
AFFECTIVE FACULTIES.—I. *Propensities:* *, alimentiveness; 1, destructiveness; 2, amativeness; 3, philoprogenitiveness; 4, adhesiveness; 5, inhabitiveness; 6, combativeness; 7, secretiveness; 8, acquisitiveness; 9, constructiveness. II. *Sentiments:* 10, cautiousness; 11, approbativeness; 12, self-esteem; 13, benevolence; 14, reverence; 15, firmness; 16, conscientiousness; 17, hope; 18, marvelousness; 19, ideality; 20, mirthfulness; 21, imitation. INTELLECTUAL FACULTIES.—I. *Perceptive:* 22, individuality; 23, configuration; 24, size; 25, weight and resistance; 26, coloring; 27, locality; 28, order; 29, calculation; 30, eventuality; 31, time; 32, tune; 33, language. II. *Reflective:* 34, comparison; 35, causality.

Thoracic viscera, with some of the abdominal viscera, showing line of the diaphragm which separates them, and outline of heart, aorta, and superior caval vein, with reference to the surface of the thorax; 1 - 10, first to tenth ribs; A, M, P, T, indicate position of aortic, mitral, pulmonary, and tricuspid valves of the heart, respectively.

External Ear, or Pinna.
1, helix; 2, fossa of antihelix, or fossa triangularis; 3, fossa of helix, or fossa scaphoidea; 4, antihelix; 5, 5, concha; 6, antitragus; 7, lobule; 8, tragus.

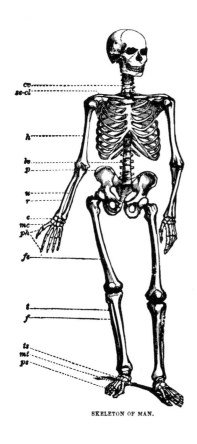

SKELETON OF MAN.

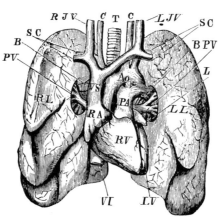

Human Lungs, Heart, and Great Vessels, front view (great vessels except of lungs cut off).

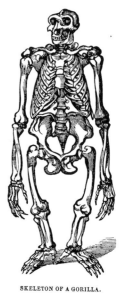

SKELETON OF A GORILLA.

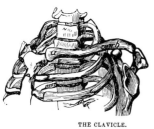

THE CLAVICLE.

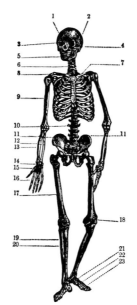

HUMAN SKELETON.

1, Frontal bone; 2, parietal bone; 3, orbit; 4, temporal bone; 5, lower jaw; 6, cervical vertebræ; 7, clavicle; 8, shoulder-blade; 9, humerus; 10, lumbar vertebræ; 11, ilium; 12, ulna; 13, radius; 14, carpus; 15, metacarpus; 16, phalanges; 17, femur; 18, datella; 19, tibia; 20, fibula; 21, tarsus; 22, metatarsus; 23, phalanges.

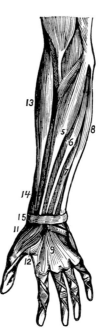

THE DORSAL SUR-FACE OF THE LEFT FOOT.

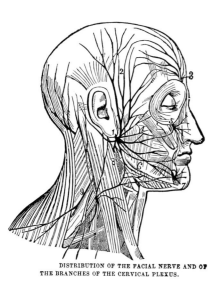

DISTRIBUTION OF THE FACIAL NERVE AND OF THE BRANCHES OF THE CERVICAL PLEXUS.

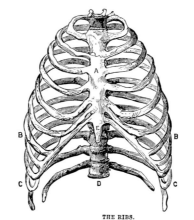

THE RIBS.

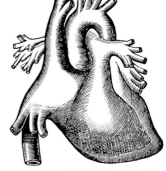

THE HEART, (RIGHT SIDE.)

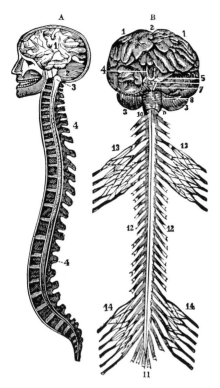

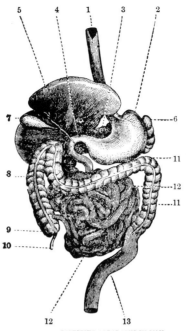

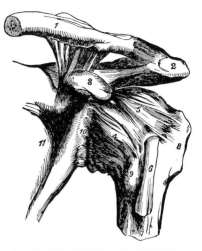

THE LEFT SHOULDER-JOINT AND ITS CONNECTIONS.

Vertebræ,

Trachea,

A. — A section of the brain and spinal column. 1. The cerebrum. 2 The cerebellum. 3. The medulla oblongata. 4, 4. The spinal cord in its canal.

B. — Anterior view of the cerebrum and spinal cord. 1, 1. The two hemispheres of the cerebrum. 2. Longitudinal fissure separating the two hemispheres. 3, 3. The cerebellum. 4. The olfactory nerve. 5. The optic nerve. 7. The third pair of nerves. 8. The pons varolii. 9. The fourth pair of nerves. 10. The lower portion of the medulla oblongata. 11. The spinal cord. 12, 12. Spinal nerves. 13, 13. The brachial plexus. 14, 14. The lumbar and sacral plexus.

DIGESTIVE APPARATUS IN MAN.

1. Gullet.	8. Large intestine.
2. Stomach.	9. Cæcum.
3. Pancreas.	10. Appendix of the cæcum.
4. Pylorus.	11. Colon.
5. Liver.	12. Small intestine.
6. Spleen.	13. Rectum.
7. Gall-bladder.	

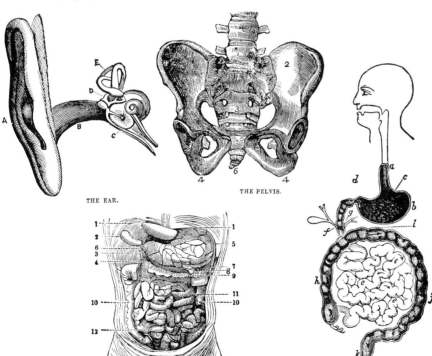

THE EAR.

THE PELVIS.

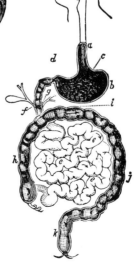

ALIMENTARY CANAL.

a, œsophagus; b, stomach; c. cardiac orifice; d, pylorus; e, small intestine; f, biliary duct; g, pancreatic duct; h, ascending colon; i. transverse colon; j, descending colon; k, rectum.

CAVITY OF THE ABDOMEN.

1. Diaphragm.	6. Pyloric end	10. Great intestine,
2. Gall-bladder.	of stomach.	(colon.)
3. Right lobe of liver.	7. Spleen.	11. Small intestine,
4. Duodenum.	8. Omentum.	(jejunum.)
5. Great end of	9. Pancreas.	12. Small intestine,
stomach.		(ileum.)

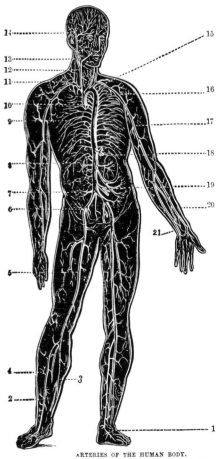

ARTERIES OF THE HUMAN BODY.

1. Tarsal.—2. Peroneal. — 3. Posterior tibial.—4. Anterior tibial. 5. Femoral. — 6. Iliac. — 7. Sacral. — 8. Renal. — 9. Intercostal. — 10. Aorta.—11. Subclavian.—12. Carotid.—13. Vertebral.—14. Temporal.—15. Curvature of the Aorta. — 16. Axillary.—17. Brachial. 18. Cœliac. — 19. Mesenteric arteries. — 20. Radial. — 21. Ulnar. See ARTERY.

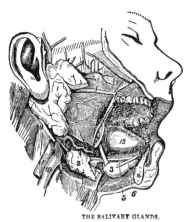

THE SALIVARY GLANDS.

1, The parotid gland ; 2, the sub-maxillary gland ; 3, the sublingual gland ; 4, Steno's duct ; 5, Wharton's duct ; 6, Bartholin's duct ; 7, masseter muscle ; 8, mastoid process ; 9, digastric muscle ; 10, internal jugular vein ; 11, external carotid artery ; 12, the tongue.

THE UPPER SURFACE OF THE TONGUE, SHOWING THE PAPILLÆ.

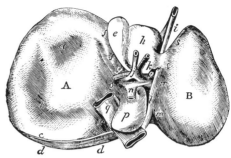

THE LIVER.

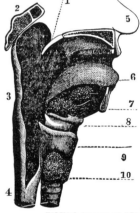

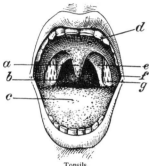

Tonsils.

a, uvula ; b, pharynx ; c, tongue ; d, palate ; e, posterior, and f, anterior pillar of the fauces, between which is g, the tonsil.

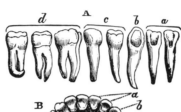

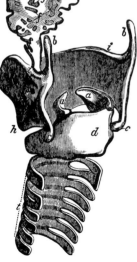

CARTILAGES OF LARYNX AND EPIGLOTTIS, AND UPPER RINGS OF TRACHEA

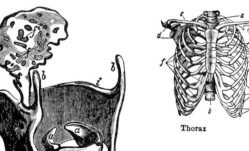

Thorax

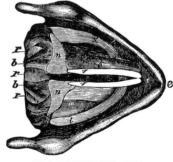

VIEW OF LARYNX FROM ABOVE.

VERTICAL SECTION OF THE MOUTH AND THROAT.

1. Pendulous palate ; 2. Base of the cranium ; 3. Pharynx ; 4. Œsophagus ; 5. Nose ; 6. Tongue ; 7. Salivary glands ; 8. Lingual bone ; 9. Thyroid gland ; 10. Trachea or windpipe.

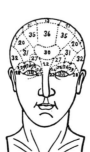

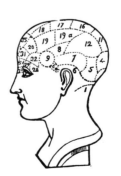

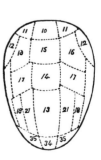

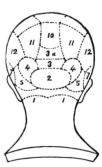

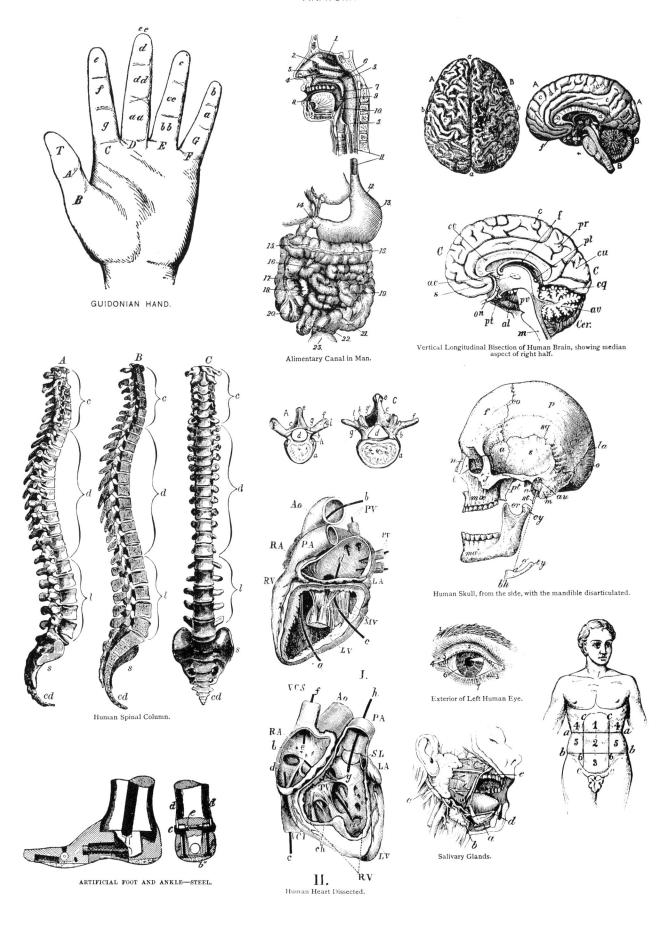

GUIDONIAN HAND.

Alimentary Canal in Man.

Vertical Longitudinal Bisection of Human Brain, showing median aspect of right half.

Human Spinal Column.

J.

II.
Human Heart Dissected.

Human Skull, from the side, with the mandible disarticulated.

Exterior of Left Human Eye.

Salivary Glands.

ARTIFICIAL FOOT AND ANKLE—STEEL.

Manx Cat

Tiger Cat

Beagle

Collie

Greyhound

Harrier

Setter

St. Bernard

Scottish Terrier

Retriever

Fox Hound

Pekingese Dog

Pointer

Onager (*Equus hemippus*).

Horse.

Zebra (*Equus* or *Hippotigris zebra*).

Dauw (*Equus burchelli*).

Bactrian Camel (*Camelus bactrianus*).

Llama.

Alpaca, or Paco (*Auchenia pacos*).

Arabian Camel, or Dromedary (*Camelus dromedarius*).

Cape Buffalo (*Bubalus caffer*).

Alpaca

Giant Kangaroo (*Macropus major*).

Kangaroo

Common or White-tailed Gnu (*Catoblepas gnu*).

Eland

Zebu (*Bos indicus*, var.).

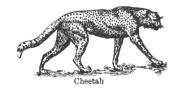
Cheetah

Jaguar (*Felis onca*).

Serval (*Felis serval*).

Leopard (*Felis pardus*).

Black Panther (a variety of *Felis pardus*).

Head of Lion (*Felis leo*), from photograph by Dixon, London.

Caracal (*Lynx caracal*).

Ocelot (*Felis pardalis*).

Chetah (*Gueparda jubata*).

Royal Tiger (*Felis tigris*).

Lynx (*Lynx canadensis*).

Leopard

Chati

Cougar

Serval

Lioness and Whelps

Ounce, or Snow-leopard (*Felis irbis*).

Musk-ox (*Ovibos moschatus*).

African Elephant (*Elephas* or *Loxodon africanus*).

Mammoth

Giraffe

Giraffe (*Giraffa camelopardalis*).

Aurochs (*Bison bonasus*).

Yak (*Poëphagus grunniens*).

Indian Elephant (*Elephas indicus*).

One-horned Rhinoceros (*Rhinoceros unicornis*).

Hippopotamus amphibius.

American Bison (*Bison americanus*).

Gazelle

Gemsbok.

Bighorn of the Rocky Mountains (*Ovis montana*).

Thian-shan (*Ovis poli*).

Rocky Mountain Goat (*Haplocerus montanus*).

Argali (*Caprovis argali*).

Sing-sing Antelope (*Kobus sing-sing*).

Wapiti, or American Elk (*Cervus canadensis*).

Reindeer (*Rangifer tarandus*).

Elk (*Alces malchis*).

Springbok

Roebuck (*Capreolus capræa*).

Wild Goat (*Capra ægagrus*).

29

Quadricorn Sheep (*Ovis aries*, var. *quadricornis*).

Alpine Ibex or Steinbok (*Capra ibex*).

Addax of Eastern Africa (*A. nasomaculatus*).

Caribou (*Rangifer caribou*).

Koodoo, or Striped Antelope (*Strepsiceros kudu*).

Blacktail, or Mule-deer (*Cariacus macrotis*).

Ravine-deer (*Tetraceros quadricornis*).

Common Buffalo (*Bubalus buffelus*).

Aoudad (*Ammotragus tragelaphus*).

Moose

Bighorn

Doe of the Virginia Deer (*Cariacus virginianus*).

Reindeer

Fighting Ram, a variety of *Ovis aries*.

Slender Loris (*Loris gracilis*).

Orang-utan *Simia satyrus*.

Gorilla (*Troglodytes gorilla* or *Gorilla savagei*).

Rhesus Monkey (*Macacus rhesus*).

Baboon

Baboon (*Cynocephalus maimon*).

CHIMPANZEE.

THE ANDAMAN MONKEY.

Chimpanzee (*Troglodytes niger*).

Chimpanzee

Deer-mouse, or White-footed Mouse (*Hesperomys leucopus*).

Sable (*Mustela zibellina*).

Guinea Pig

Hamster

Unau, or Two-toed Sloth (*Cholopus didactylus*).

European Badger (*Meles vulgaris*).

American Sable or Pine-marten (*Mustela americana*).

Deer-mouse, or Jumping-mouse (*Zapus hudsonius*).

Tasmanian Devil

Aye-aye (*Daubentonia madagascariensis*).

Ring-tailed Bassaris (*Bassaris astuta*).

Meadow-mouse (*Arvicola riparius*).

Bruang (*Helarctos malayanus*).

Spectacled Bear (*Tremarctos ornatus*).

American Black Bear (*Ursus americanus*).

Polar Bear (*Ursus maritimus*).

Æluropus melanoleucus.

Grizzly Bear (*Ursus horribilis*).

Koala (*Phascolarctos cinereus*).

Painted Hyena, or Hunting-dog (*Lycaon pictus*).

Black-backed Jackal (*Canis mesomelas*).

Spotted Hyena (*Hyæna crocuta* or *Crocuta maculata*).

Buansuah (*Cyon primævus*).

Dingo (*Canis dingo*).

Coyote (*Canis latrans*).

Wolf

Common Wolf (*Canis lupus*)

33

Woodchuck (*Arctomys monax*).

Common Opossum (*Didelphys virginiana*).

Marmose (*Didelphys dorsigera*).

Wart-hog (*Phacochœrus africanus*).

Malay Tapir (*Tapirus malayanus*).

Beaver (*Castor fiber*).

Conepatl (*Conepatus mapurito*).

Wild Boar (*Sus scrofa*).

American Tapir (*Tapirus americanus*).

Common Skunk (*Mephitis mephitica*).

Wolverene or Carcajou (*Gulo luscus*).

Four-toed Ant-bear (*Tamandua tetradactyla*).

Porcupine

Common Racoon (*Procyon lotor*).

34

Red Fox (*Vulpes vulgaris* or *fulvus*).

Kit-fox (*Vulpes velox*).

Gray Fox (*Urocyon virginianus*).

Fox

Brown Mouse-lemur (*Chirogaleus milii*).

Gold-mole (*Chrysochloris aureus*).

Northern Sea-lion (*Eumetopias stelleri*).

Mongoose

Otary (*Otaria forsteri*).

Poyou

Californian Sea-lion (*Zalophus californianus*).

Pacific or Cook's Walrus (*Trichechus* or *Rosmarus obesus*).

Ribbon-seal (*Histriophoca fasciata*).

Flying Squirrel

Aard-vark

Jerboa

South American Chincha or Rabbit-squirrel (*Lagidium cuvieri*).

Chinchilla lanigera.

Schizodon fuscus.

Kangaroo-rat (*Dipodomys phillipsi*).

Cotton-rat (*Sigmodon hispidus*).

Jack-rabbit (*Lepus callotis*).

Cottontail, or Wood-rabbit (*Lepus sylvaticus*).

American Varying Hare (*Lepus americanus*).

Florida Wood-rat (*Neotoma floridana*).

Flying-lemur (*Galeopithecus volans*).

Rice-field Mouse (*Oryzomys palustris*).

Mouse (*Mus musculus*).

Chickaree, or Red Squirrel (*Sciurus hudsonius*).

Chipmunk (*Tamias striatus*).

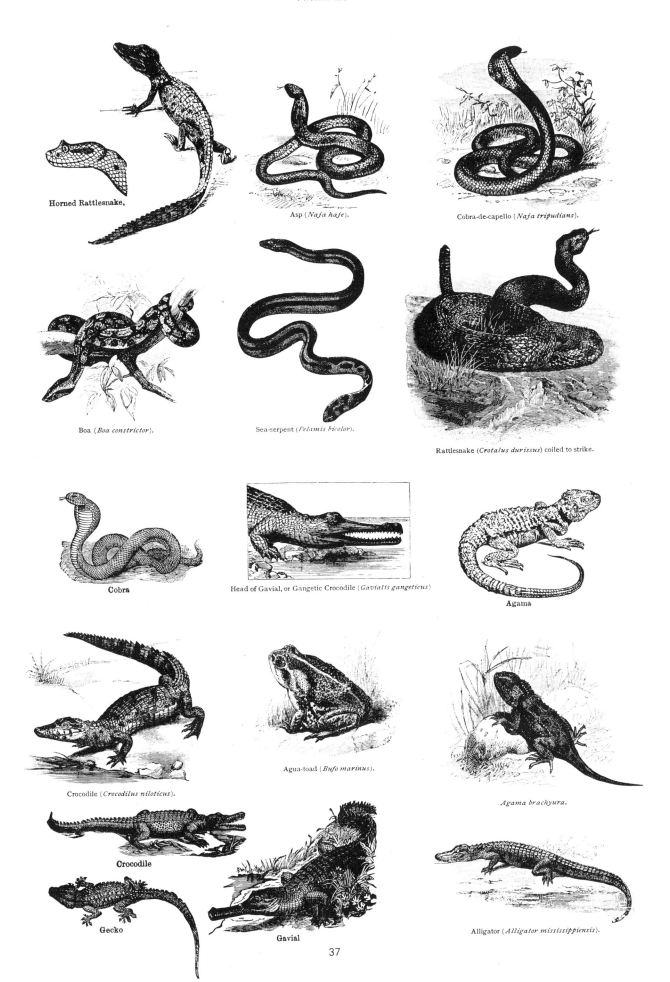

Horned Rattlesnake,

Asp (*Naja haje*).

Cobra-de-capello (*Naja tripudians*).

Boa (*Boa constrictor*).

Sea-serpent (*Pelamis bicolor*).

Rattlesnake (*Crotalus durissus*) coiled to strike.

Cobra

Head of Gavial, or Gangetic Crocodile (*Gavialis gangeticus*)

Agama

Crocodile (*Crocodilus niloticus*).

Agua-toad (*Bufo marinus*).

Agama brachyura.

Crocodile

Gecko

Gavial

Alligator (*Alligator mississippiensis*).

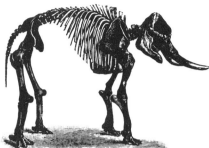

Mastodon (*Mastodon giganteus*).

Medieval Architecture of the best period.—West front of Amiens Cathedral, France; 13th century.

Gate-house.— Porte de Joigny, Vitré, France.

Domical Church.— Cathedral of Périgueux, France; 11th century.

Triumphal Arch.— Arch of Constantine, Rome.

Blind-story.— Triforium of Lincoln Cathedral.

Triple Window, Medieval Geometric style of middle of 13th century.— Lincoln Cathedral, England.

Galleries of the west front of the Cathedral of Amiens, 13th century, illustrating treatment of galleries as a decorative feature. (From Viollet-le-Duc's "Dict. de l'Architecture.")

Bretesses.
(From Viollet-le-Duc's "Dict. de l'Architecture.")

Rose-window in North Transept of Abbey Church of Saint Denis, France.

Atlantes.
Otto Heinrich's Palace, Heidelberg Castle, Baden.

Remains of Amphitheater of Nîmes, France.

Rococo.— An interior in Schloss Bruchsal, Baden, Germany. (From "L'Art pour Tous.")

Early English Architecture.— Galilee Porch and South Transept of Lincoln Cathedral.

Bridge-tower.— Moldau Bridge, Prague, Bohemia.

Chinese Art.— The Fuhkien Temple, Ningpo.

Romanesque.— Great Doorway of the Abbey Church of Vézelay, 12th century. (From Viollet-le-Duc's " Dict. de l'Architecture.")

A   B
Broaches.
A, southwest tower, Cathedral of Bayeux, Normandy; B, Church of St. Nicholas, Walcot, England.

Choir-screen, Cathedral of Lincoln, England.

Anamorphosis.

Russo-Byzantine Architecture.— Cathedral of the Assumption, Kremlin, Moscow.

THE PARTHENON

Dais.— Throne-room, Windsor Castle, England.

Atrium.—Restoration of a Pompeiian interior.

Reredos and Altar of Lichfield Cathedral, England.

French Roof.— Pavilion of Women's Hospital, New York City.

Wall-tower, 13th century.— Fortifications of Carcassonne, France.
(From Viollet-le-Duc's "Dict. de l'Architecture.")

Screen.— Lady Chapel of Gloucester Cathedral, England,
looking toward the nave.

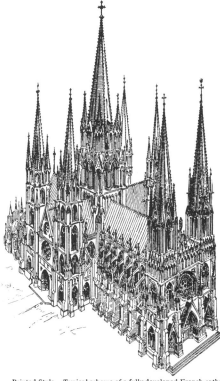

Pointed Style.—Typical scheme of a fully developed French cathedral of the 13th century. (From Viollet-le-Duc's "Dict. de l'Architecture.")

East River Suspension-bridge, New York.

Log Cabin.

Antic, Amiens Cathedral, 13th century. (From Viollet-le-Duc's "Dict. de l'Architecture.")

GOPURA,
(or gate leading into the inclosure of the temple at Seringham.)

Church at Austerfield, Bradford's Birthplace.

MONT ST. MICHEL.

Jain Architecture.—Temple at Kali Katraha, India.

ST. PAUL'S CATHEDRAL.

ST. GEORGE'S CHAPEL (N. aisle), WINDSOR.

CHURCH OF THE PILGRIMS, (Brooklyn.)

CATHEDRAL OF REIMS.

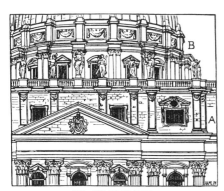

Attic of St. Peter's, Rome.
A, attic of the main edifice ; *B*, attic of the dome.

Ancient High Altar of Notre Dame, Paris, 13th century.
(Viollet-le-Duc's " Dict. de l'Architecture.")

South Aisle of Rouen Cathedral (13th century).

Altar-tomb of Philip the Bold, Duke of Burgundy, Dijon.

Remains of Amphitheater of Arles, France.

Arabic Architecture.— Tombs of the Califs, Cairo.

Doric Order.—Temple of Castor and Pollux (so called),Girgenti,Sicily.

Belfry of the Duomo in Pisa, Italy : commonly called the
Leaning Tower.

Rood-steeple. — Cathedral of Notre Dame, Paris, from the southeast.

Gate-tower or Barbican, Walmgate Bar, York, England.

The Acropolis of Athens, from the southeast.

Ionic Architecture.—Temple of Wingless Victory, on the Acropolis of Athens.

CATHEDRAL OF ULM.

Lich-gate.

ST. PATRICK'S CATHEDRAL, (Dublin.)

BAPTISTERY OF PISA, (12th century.)

STRASBURG CATHEDRAL.

CANTERBURY CATHEDRAL, (West Front.)

Italian Architecture.—Church of Sta. Maria della Salute, Venice; constructed 1632.

ANTWERP CATHEDRAL.

Hexastyle Front of the ancient Roman temple called the Maison Carrée, at Nimes, France.

MASONIC TEMPLE.

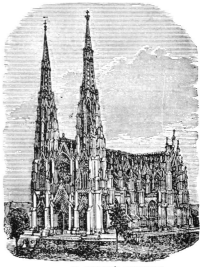

ST. PATRICK'S CATHEDRAL.

TOWER OF LITTLE SAXHAM CHURCH, SUFFOLK, (England.) (A. D. 1160.)

TEMPLE OF KYLAS ("THE PARADISE"). (Ellora.)

ST. BURKHARDT'S CHURCH, WURZBURG.

1866. — ST. BASIL'S CHURCH, (Moscow.)

A GREEK CHURCH.

HARVARD CHURCH.

NOTRE DAME DE PARIS.

TYPES OF ODD AND ANCIENT DWELLINGS.

1. Roman. 2. Cliff dwelling (aboriginal American). 3. Egyptian. 4. Assyrian American.) 5. Turkish hut. 6. Aztec. 7. Teutonic hut. 8. Sudanese. 9. Communal dwelling of Pueblo Indians. 10, 11. Hebrew house and hut. 12. Persian. 13. Hindu. 14. Peruvian. 15. Byzantine. 16. Laplander's hut. 17. Chinese. 18. North American Indian. 19. Greek.

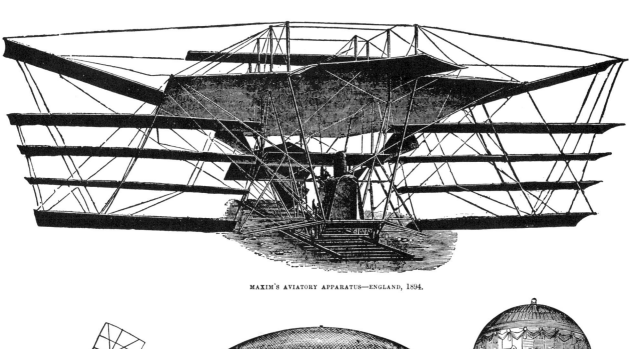

MAXIM'S AVIATORY APPARATUS—ENGLAND, 1894.

Aërodrome

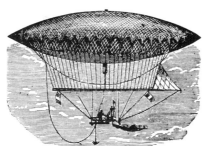

GIFFARD'S BALLOON.—1852.

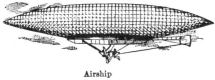

Airship

Balloons

Aëroplane

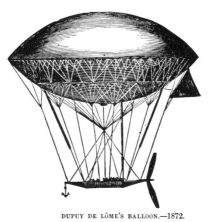

DUPUY DE LÔME'S BALLOON.—1872.

Parachute

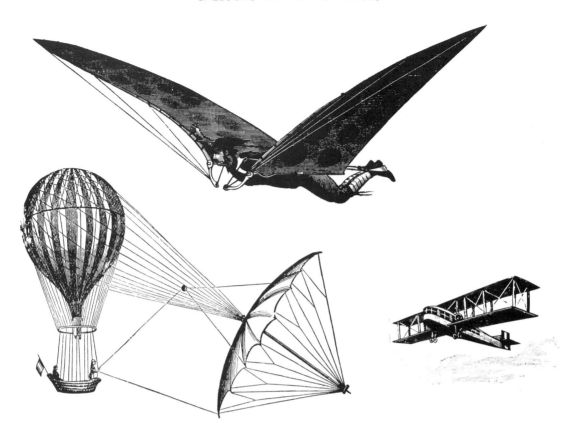

PILCHER'S FLYING MACHINE—SCOTLAND, 1895.

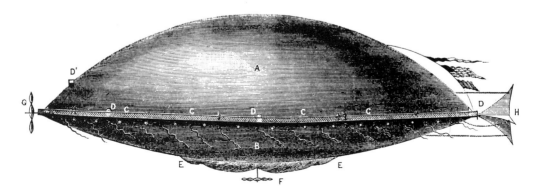

Merlin (*Falco æsalon* or *Æsalon regulus*).

Sea-eagle (*Haliaëtus pelagicus*).

Bald Eagle (*Haliaëtus leucocephalus*).

California Condor (*Cathartes californianus*).

Chanting Hawk (*Melierax musicus*).

Raven (*Corvus corax*).

Eared Vulture (*Otogyps auricularis*).

Snake-buzzard (*Circaëtus gallicus*).

Common Gray Partridge (*Perdix cinerea*).

Western Grebe (*Æchmophorus occidentalis*).

Bob-white, or Common Quail of America (*Ortyx virginiana*).

Argus-pheasant.

Gray Parrot (*Psittacus erythacus*).

Cockatoo (*Cacatua chrysolopha*).

Love-birds (*Agapornis cana*).

Virginia Horned Owl (*Bubo virginianus*).

Zebra Grass-parrakeet (*Melopsittacus undulatus*).

Ariel Toucan (*Rhamphastos ariel*).

Bird of Paradise (*Paradisea apoda*).

Tanygnathus megalorhynchus.

Snow-owl (*Nyctea scandiaca*).

Hawk-owl (*Surnia ulula*).

Peacock (*Pavo cristatus*).

Domestic Pigeon, homing variety.

Blue Jay (*Cyanocitta cristata*).

Red-headed Woodpecker (*Melanerpes erythrocephalus*)

Cardinal-bird (*Cardinalis virginianus*).

Rock-swift (*Panyptila melanoleuca*).

Hedge-sparrow (*Accentor modularis*).

American Robin (*Merula migratoria*).

Pipit, or Titlark (*Anthus ludovicianus*).

Belted Kingfisher (*Ceryle alcyon*).

Mocking-bird (*Mimus polyglottus*).

Tantalus ibis and Head of *Tantalus loculator*.

Helmet-quail (*Lophortyx californicus*).

Common Pheasant (*Phasianus colchicus*).

Canvasbacks (*Fuligula (Aristonetta) vallisneria*).

Mallard (*Anas boscas*).

Galloperdix lunulatus.

Canada Grouse (*Canace canadensis*).

Sheldrake (*Tadorna cornuta* or *vulpanser*).

Snow-goose (*Chen hyperboreus*).

Canada Goose (*Bernicla canadensis*).

One of the *Odontophorinæ* or American Partridges (*Dendrortyx macrurus*).

Scaled Quail (*Callipepla squamata*).

Ocellated Turkey (*Meleagris ocellata*).

European White Swan (*Cygnus olor*).

Roseate Spoonbill (*Ajaja rosea*).

A Male Ostrich (*Struthio camelus*).

Head of *Phœnicopterus antiquorum*, one of the *Odontoglossæ*.

Great Blue Heron (*Ardea herodias*).

Brown Pelican (*Pelecanus fuscus*).

White Stork (*Ciconia alba*).

Agami, or Trumpeter (*Psophia crepitans*).

Furia horrens.

Long-eared Bat (*Barbastellus communis*).

Razorbill (*Alca torda*), in winter plumage.

THE BELTED KINGFISHER.

South American Ostrich (*Rhea americana*).

Marsh-hawk, or Harrier (*Circus hudsonius*).

Brent-goose (*Bernicla brenta*).

Barn-owl (*Aluco flammeus*).

Barred Owl (*Strix nebulosa*).

Marsh-Blackbird (*Agelæus tricolor*).

Columba.— French, 12th century. (From Viollet-le-Duc's "Dict.
du Mobilier français.")

54

Yellow-headed Blackbird

Guinea Fowl

Turtledove

Pelican

Macaw

Bald Eagle

Prairie Chicken

Rhea

Moa

Gull,

Secretary-bird (*Serpentarius secretarius*).

Flamingo

Acadian Owl

Auk

Red-legged Partridge (*Caccabis rufa*).

Sharp-shinned Hawk (*Accipiter fuscus*); adult female.

Turkey-buzzard (*Cathartes aura*).

Rough-legged Buzzard (*Archibuteo lagopus*).

American Snake-bird (*Plotus anhinga*).

Cockatoo

Bobwhite

Wild Goose

Mallard

Teal

Wood Duck

Ocellated Turkey

Ruddy Duck

Thrush

Waxwing

Turkeys

Owl

Junco

Laughing Jackass

Snowy Owl

Ruffed Grouse

Ruby-throated Humming Bird

Robins

Kittiwake

Shoebill

Saddle-billed Stork

Puffin

Snipe

Lammergeier

Ostrich

Tody

Quail.

Stork.

56

BRIDGES

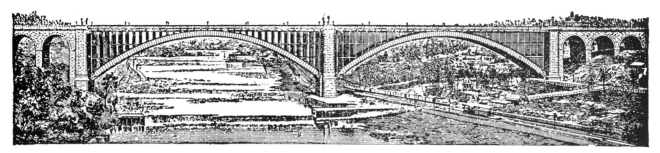

THE WASHINGTON BRIDGE OVER HARLEM RIVER.

THE RIALTO.

ROMAN AQUEDUCT, (*Pont-du-Gard.*)

THE GATE OF OLD LONDON BRIDGE.
(Copied from Visscher's View in 1579.)

CANTILEVER RAILROAD BRIDGE AT NIAGARA.

THE BRIDGE OF SIGHS (VENICE).

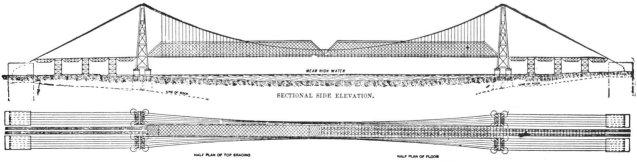

SECTIONAL SIDE ELEVATION.

HALF PLAN OF TOP BRACING   HALF PLAN OF FLOOR

NEW YORK AND JERSEY CITY SUSPENSION BRIDGE, BEGUN IN 1897.

CITIES

First Settlement at Albany.

SAVANNAH IN 1850.

MONTEVIDEO.

GARDEN OF GETHSEMANE, AND MOUNT OF OLIVES.

INTERLACHEN.

RIO DE JANEIRO.

GHENT.

The Chew House at Germantown.

NEW YORK IN 1664.

VIEW OF CONSTANTINOPLE AT THE END OF
THE 17TH CENTURY.

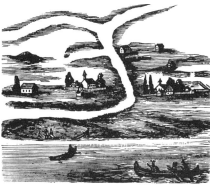

CHICAGO IN 1830.

STOCKHOLM.

PORTLAND.

ACAPULCO.

BAR GATE, (Southampton.)

CITY OF MOROCCO.

JERICHO.

AUGSBURG.

JERUSALEM.

COPENHAGEN—THE GREAT SQUARE.

QUEBEC.

FLORENCE, (from San Miniato.)

MADISON.

WHEELING IN 1860.

1. The Rœmerberg.   2. The Taxis Palace.

FRANKFORT.

GAZA.

SAMARIA.

NEW YORK FROM FORT RICHMOND.

THE KREMLIN.

NUREMBERG.

Palisaded Town.

ENTRANCE OF MODERN NAZARETH.

Windmill.
a, frame ; *b*, sails ; *c*, vane ; *d*, pump-rod.

Barley.

Gang-plow.
a, rear plow ; *a'*, front plow ; *b*, long beam ; *b'*, short beam ; *c*, wheel running on land ; *c'*, wheel running in furrow ; *d*, lever ; *e*, seat ; *f*, ratchet-adjusting lever ; *g*, pole.

Wheat (*Triticum sativum*).

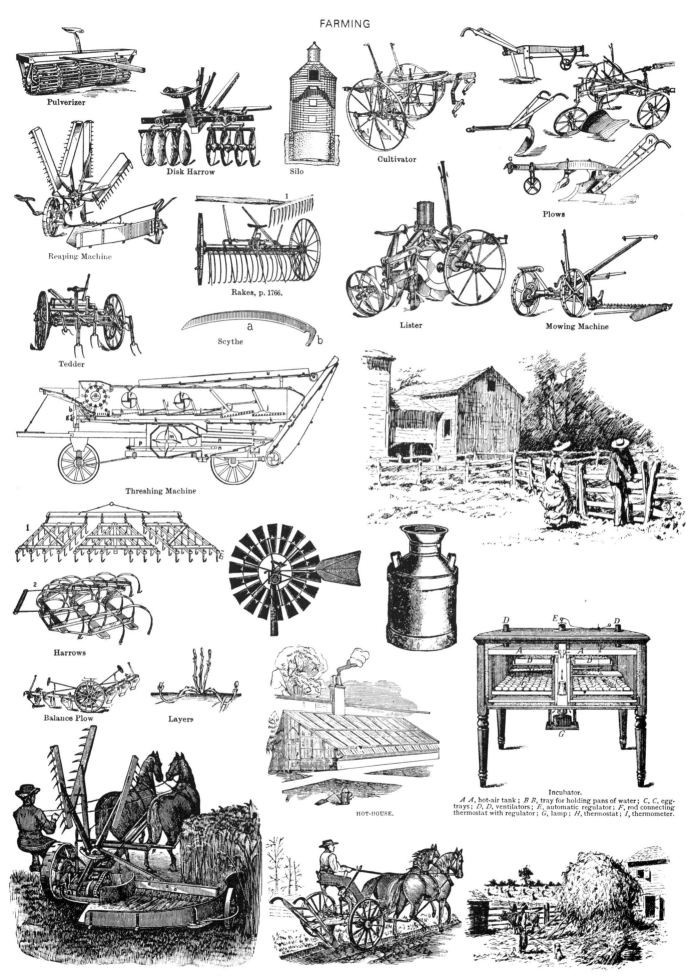

Pulverizer

Disk Harrow

Silo

Cultivator

Plows

Reaping Machine

Rakes, p. 1766.

Lister

Mowing Machine

Tedder

Scythe

Threshing Machine

Harrows

Balance Plow

Layers

HOT-HOUSE.

Incubator.
A A, hot-air tank ; B B, tray for holding pans of water ; C, C, egg-trays ; D, D, ventilators ; E, automatic regulator ; F, rod connecting thermostat with regulator ; G, lamp ; H, thermostat ; I, thermometer.

Striped Bass

Black Bass

Thresher Shark

Sucker

Alaskan

Trout

Surgeon Fish

Rudd

Caribe

Sharks

Salmon

a

Saury

Surf Fish

Smelt

Sea Bass

Thread Herring

Sting Ray

Pike

Sailfish

Pollack

Sardine

Dollarfish

Sailor's-choice

Flying Fish

Sculpin

Herring

Quinnat Salmon

Rainbow Trout

Ribbon Fish

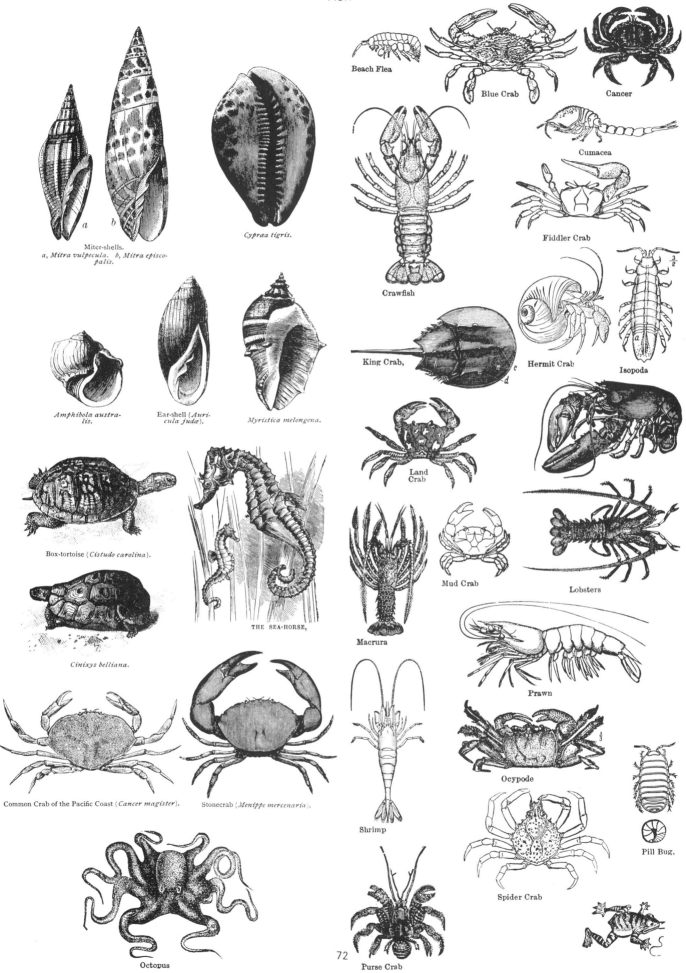

Miter-shells.
a, Mitra vulpecula. b, Mitra episco-palis.

Cypræa tigris.

Beach Flea

Blue Crab

Cancer

Cumacea

Crawfish

Fiddler Crab

Amphibola austra-lis.

Ear-shell (*Auri-cula judæ*).

Myristica melongena.

King Crab,

Hermit Crab

Isopoda

Land Crab

Box-tortoise (*Cistudo carolina*).

THE SEA-HORSE,

Macrura

Mud Crab

Lobsters

Cinixys belliana.

Prawn

Common Crab of the Pacific Coast (*Cancer magister*).

Stonecrab (*Menippe mercenaria*).

Shrimp

Ocypode

Pill Bug,

Spider Crab

Octopus

72

Purse Crab

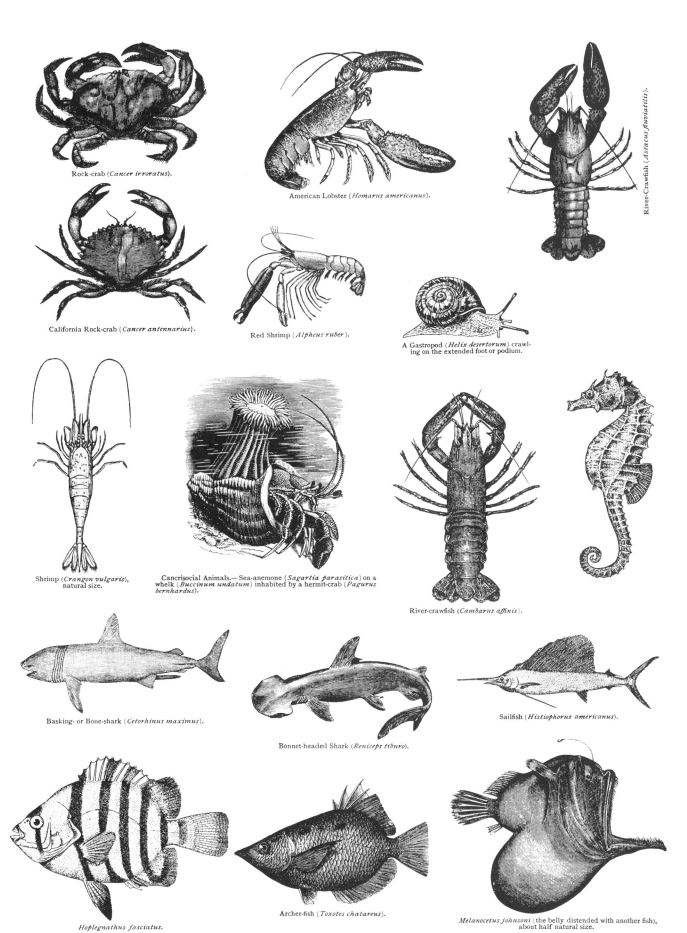

Rock-crab (*Cancer irroratus*).

American Lobster (*Homarus americanus*).

River-Crawfish (*Astacus fluviatilis*).

California Rock-crab (*Cancer antennarius*).

Red Shrimp (*Alpheus ruber*).

A Gastropod (*Helix desertorum*) crawling on the extended foot or podium.

Shrimp (*Crangon vulgaris*), natural size.

Cancrisocial Animals.— Sea-anemone (*Sagartia parasitica*) on a whelk (*Buccinum undatum*) inhabited by a hermit-crab (*Pagurus bernhardus*).

River-crawfish (*Cambarus affinis*).

Basking- or Bone-shark (*Cetorhinus maximus*).

Bonnet-headed Shark (*Reniceps tiburo*).

Sailfish (*Histiophorus americanus*).

Hoplegnathus fasciatus.

Archer-fish (*Toxotes chatareus*).

Melanocetus johnsoni (the belly distended with another fish), about half natural size.

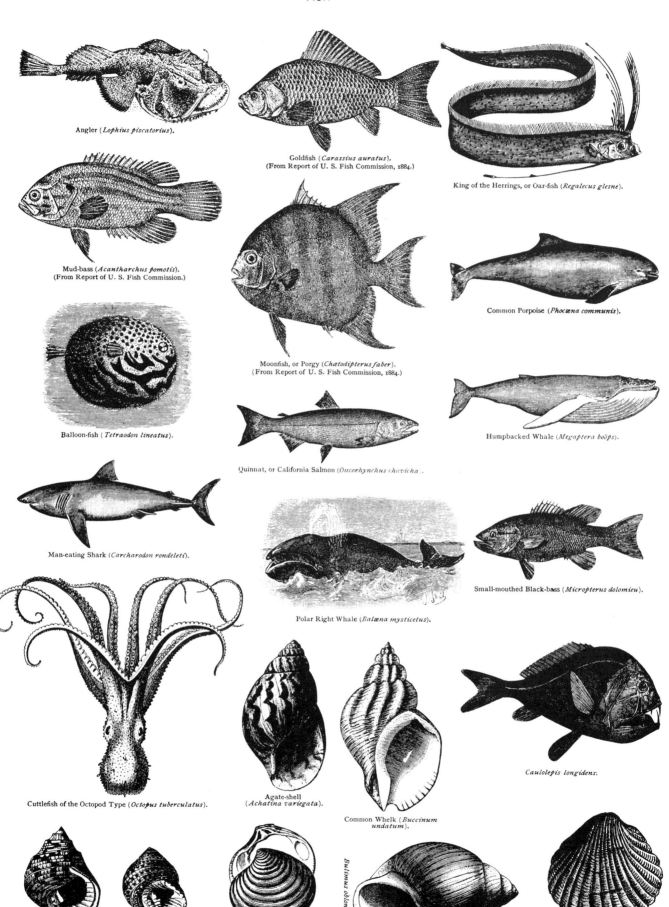

Angler (*Lophius piscatorius*).

Goldfish (*Carassius auratus*).
(From Report of U. S. Fish Commission, 1884.)

King of the Herrings, or Oar-fish (*Regalecus glesne*).

Mud-bass (*Acantharchus pomotis*).
(From Report of U. S. Fish Commission.)

Common Porpoise (*Phocæna communis*).

Balloon-fish (*Tetraodon lineatus*).

Moonfish, or Porgy (*Chætodipterus faber*).
(From Report of U. S. Fish Commission, 1884.)

Humpbacked Whale (*Megaptera boöps*).

Quinnat, or California Salmon (*Oncorhynchus chavicha*).

Man-eating Shark (*Carcharodon rondeleti*).

Small-mouthed Black-bass (*Micropterus dolomieu*).

Polar Right Whale (*Balæna mysticetus*).

Cuttlefish of the Octopod Type (*Octopus tuberculatus*).

Agate-shell
(*Achatina variegata*).

Common Whelk (*Buccinum undatum*).

Caulolepis longidens.

Monodonta labio.

Monodonta (Clanculus) pharaonis.

Astarte sulcata.

Bulimus oblongus.

Common Cockle (*Cardium edule*).

Accubation.—An ancient dinner.

Lobsters

Apostle-Spoons.

Chop-sticks.

1, Ale-yard.
2, Tricky Ale-yard.

MOLASSES

COFFEE

FLOUR

HYSON

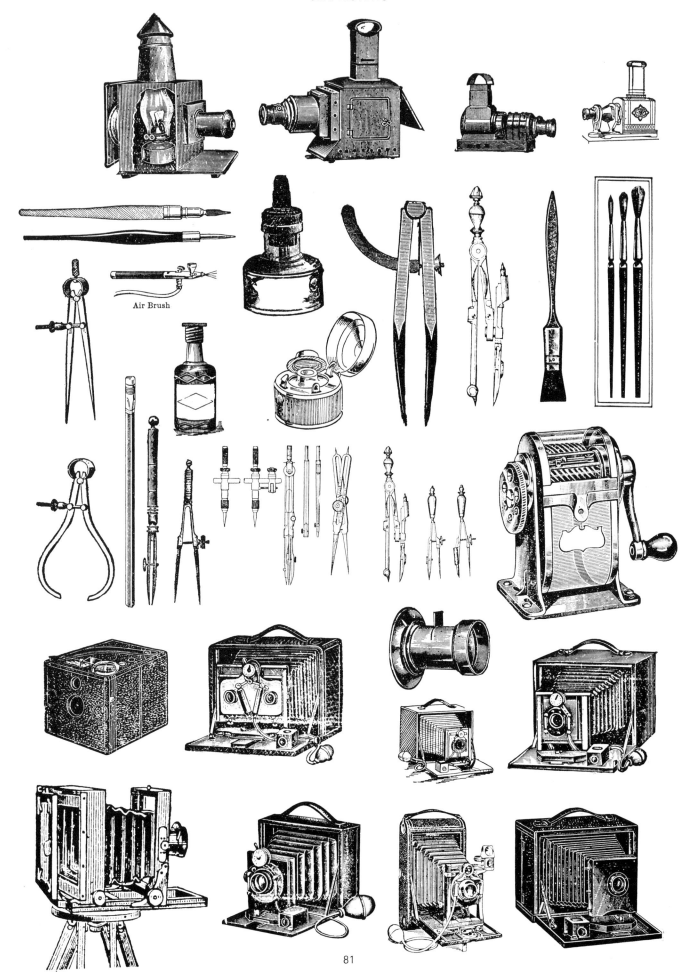

Air Brush

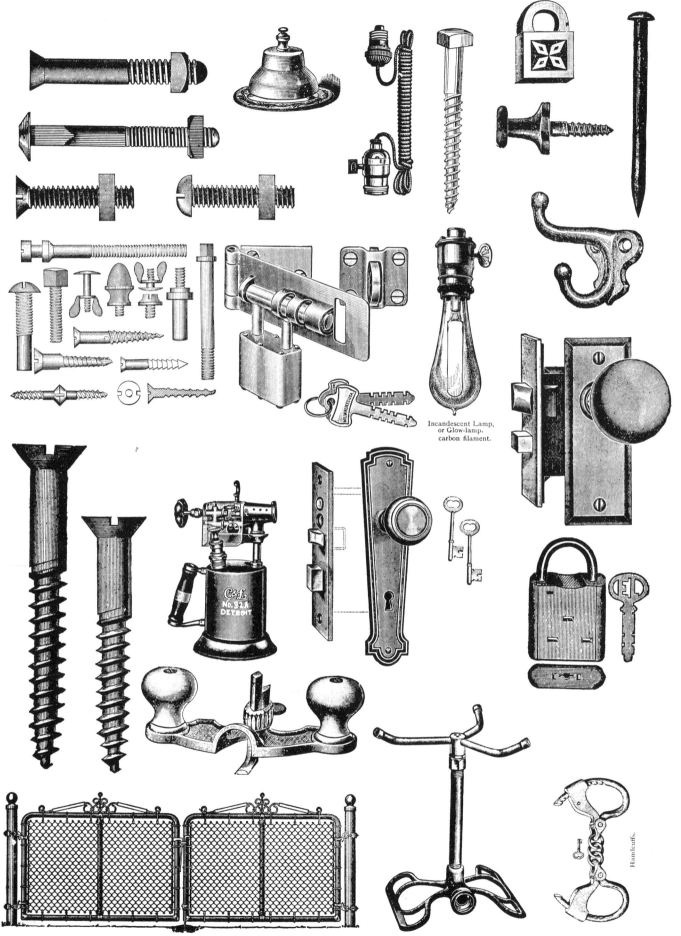

Incandescent Lamp,
or Glow-lamp.
carbon filament.

Handcuffs.

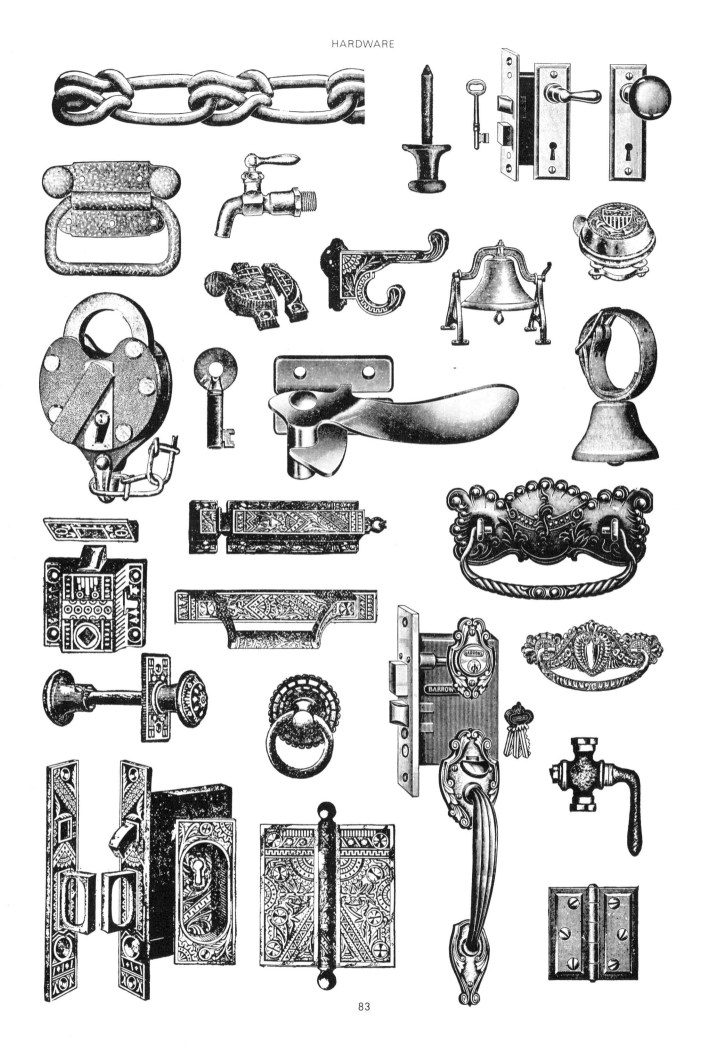

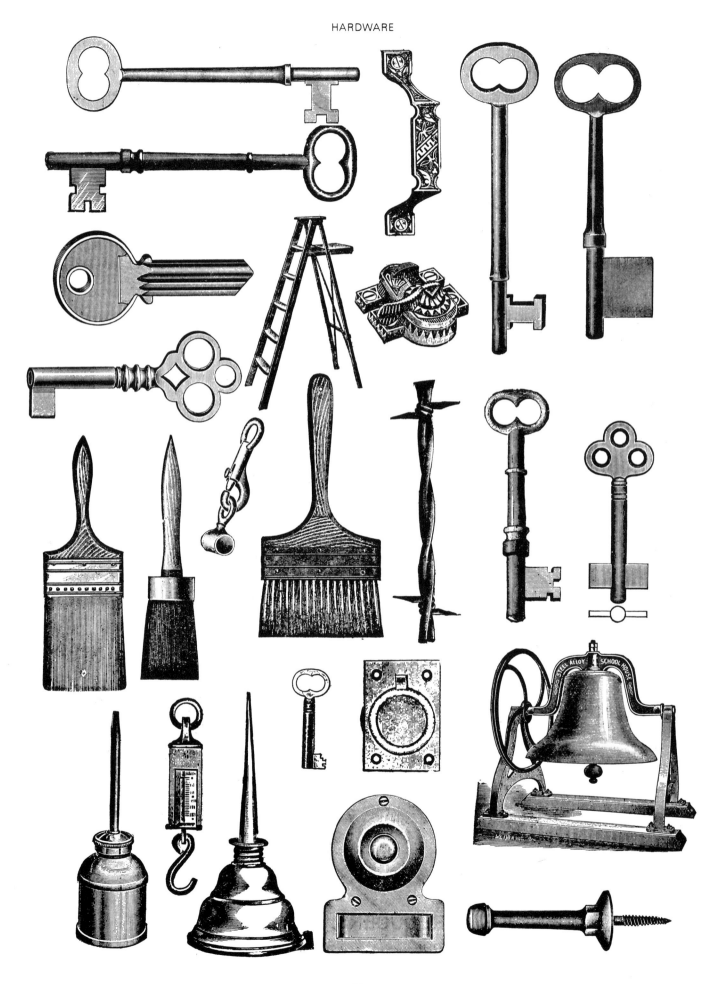

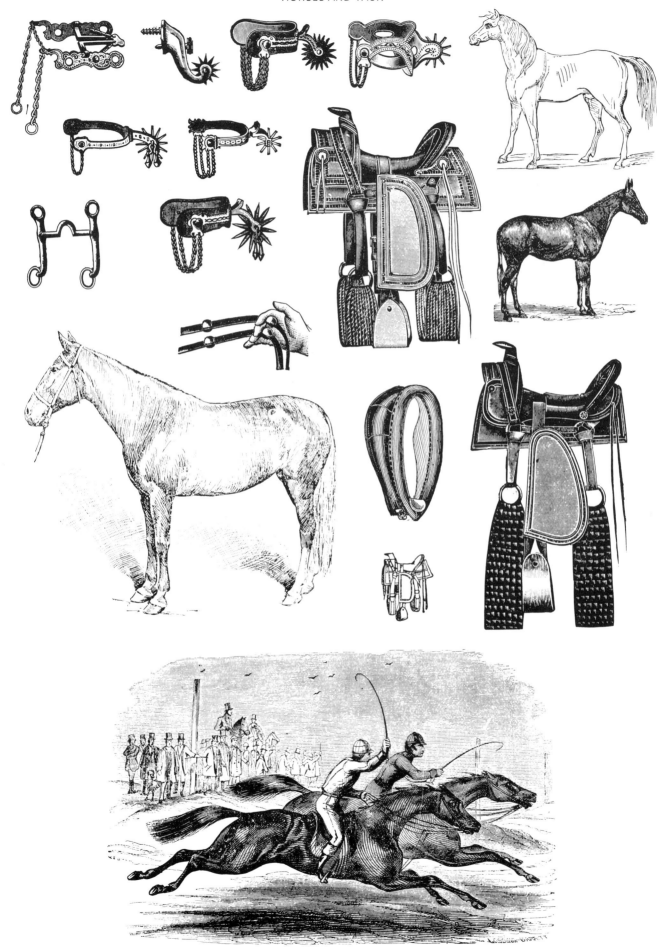

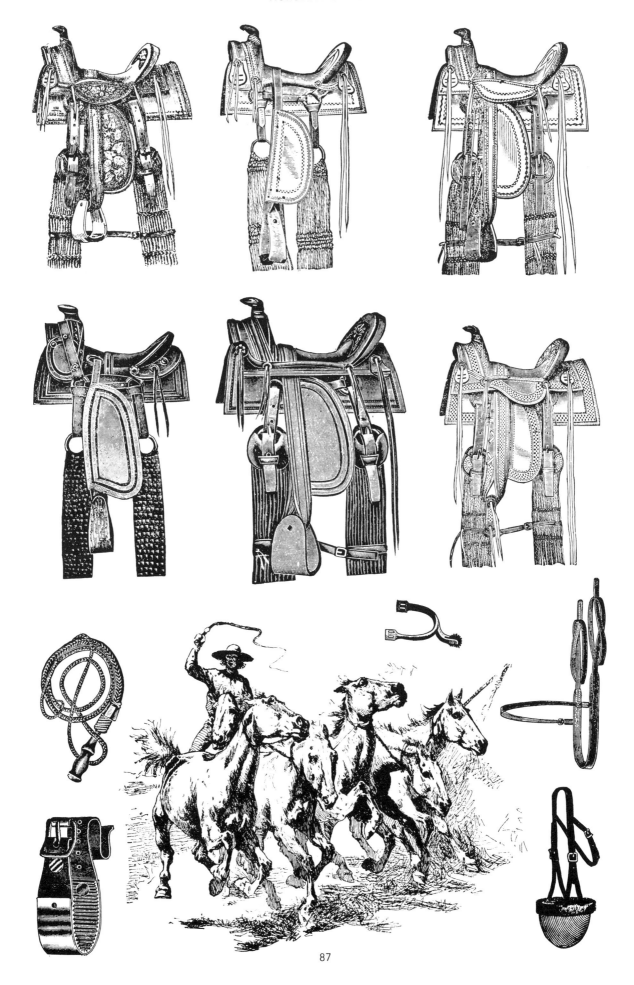

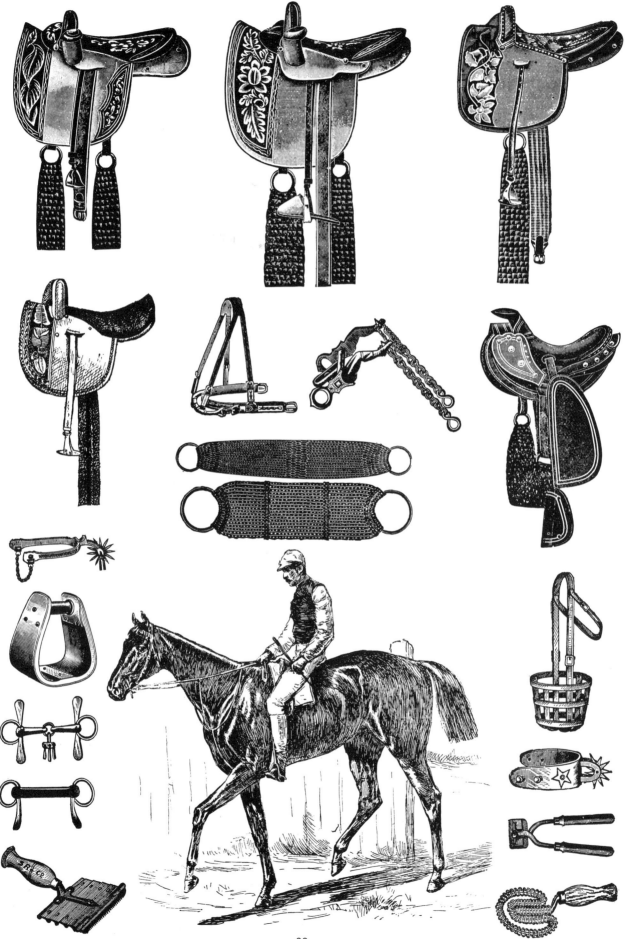

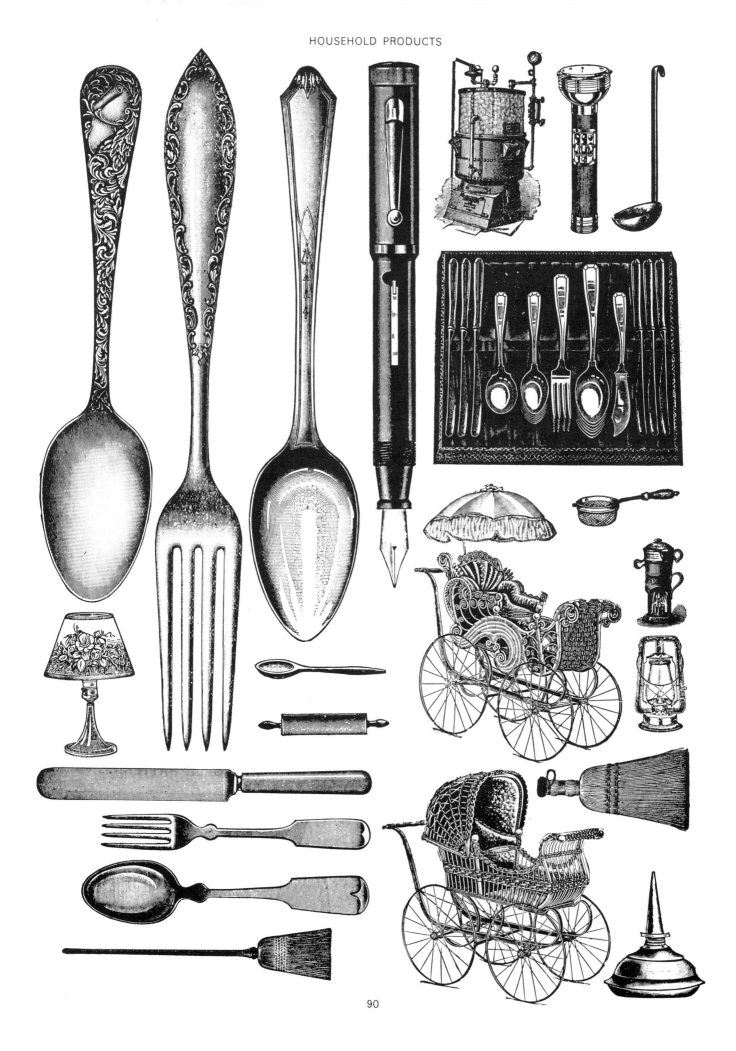

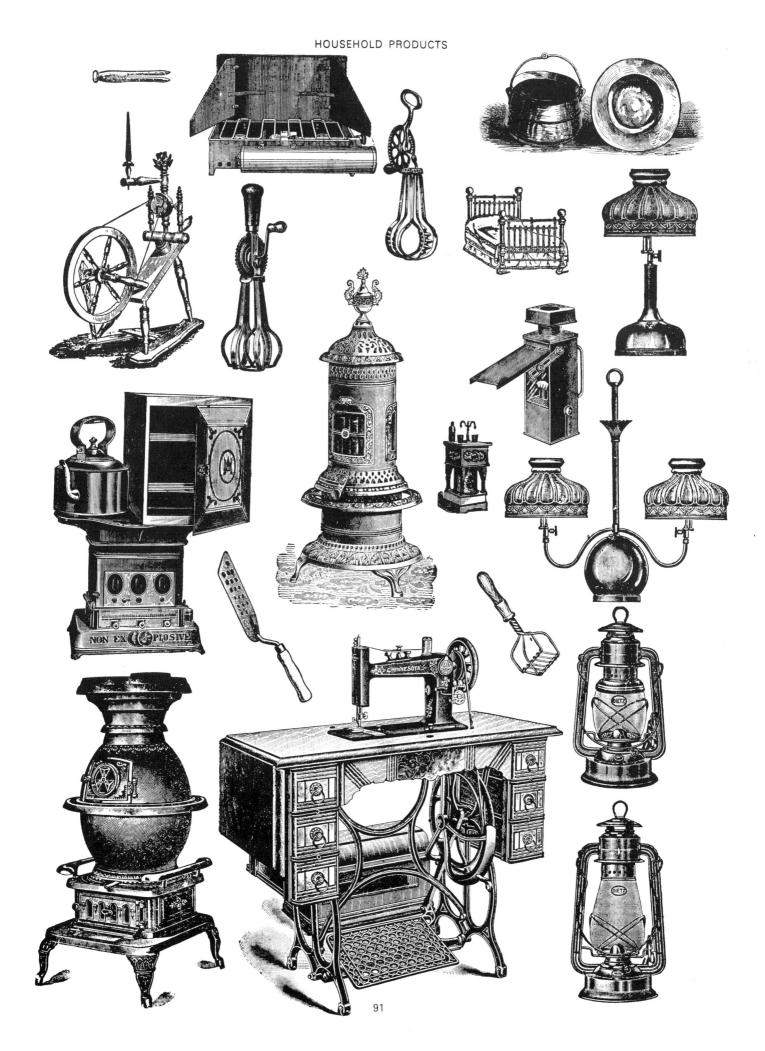

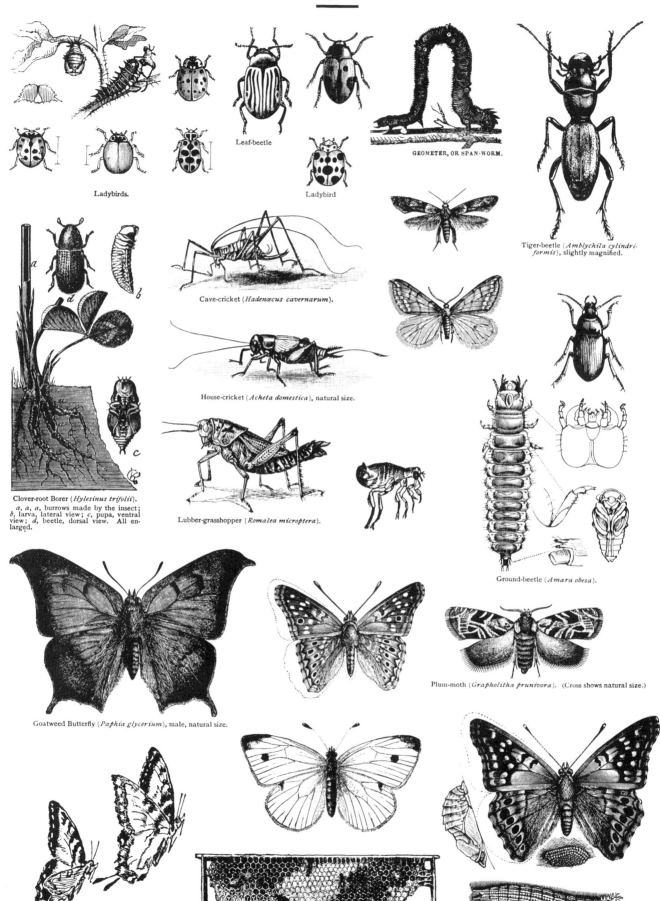

Ladybirds.

Leaf-beetle

Ladybird

GEOMETER, OR SPAN-WORM.

Tiger-beetle (*Amblychila cylindriformis*), slightly magnified.

Cave-cricket (*Hadenœcus cavernarum*).

House-cricket (*Acheta domestica*), natural size.

Clover-root Borer (*Hylesinus trifolii*).
a, a, a, burrows made by the insect; *b*, larva, lateral view; *c*, pupa, ventral view; *d*, beetle, dorsal view. All enlarged.

Lubber-grasshopper (*Romalea microptera*).

Ground-beetle (*Amara obesa*).

Goatweed Butterfly (*Paphia glycerium*), male, natural size.

Plum-moth (*Grapholitha prunivora*). (Cross shows natural size.)

Tawny Emperor (*Apatura herse*).

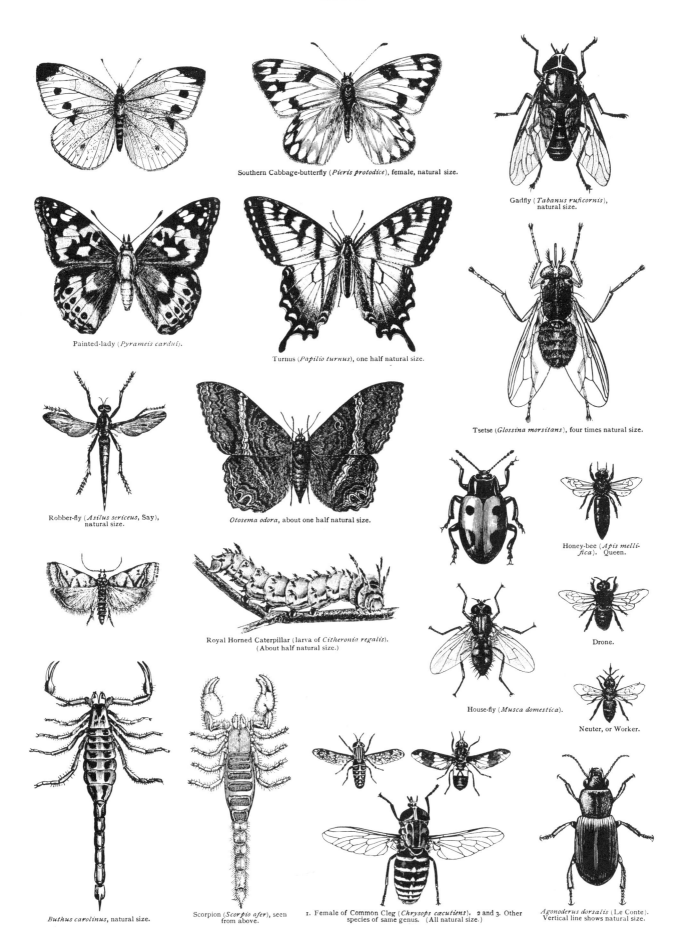

Southern Cabbage-butterfly (*Pieris protodice*), female, natural size.

Gadfly (*Tabanus ruficornis*), natural size.

Painted-lady (*Pyrameis cardui*).

Turnus (*Papilio turnus*), one half natural size.

Tsetse (*Glossina morsitans*), four times natural size.

Robber-fly (*Asilus sericeus*, Say), natural size.

Otosema odora, about one half natural size.

Honey-bee (*Apis melli-fica*). Queen.

Royal Horned Caterpillar (larva of *Citheronia regalis*). (About half natural size.)

House-fly (*Musca domestica*).

Drone.

Neuter, or Worker.

Buthus carolinus, natural size.

Scorpion (*Scorpio afer*), seen from above.

1. Female of Common Cleg (*Chrysops cacutiens*). 2 and 3. Other species of same genus. (All natural size.)

Agonoderus dorsalis (Le Conte). Vertical line shows natural size.

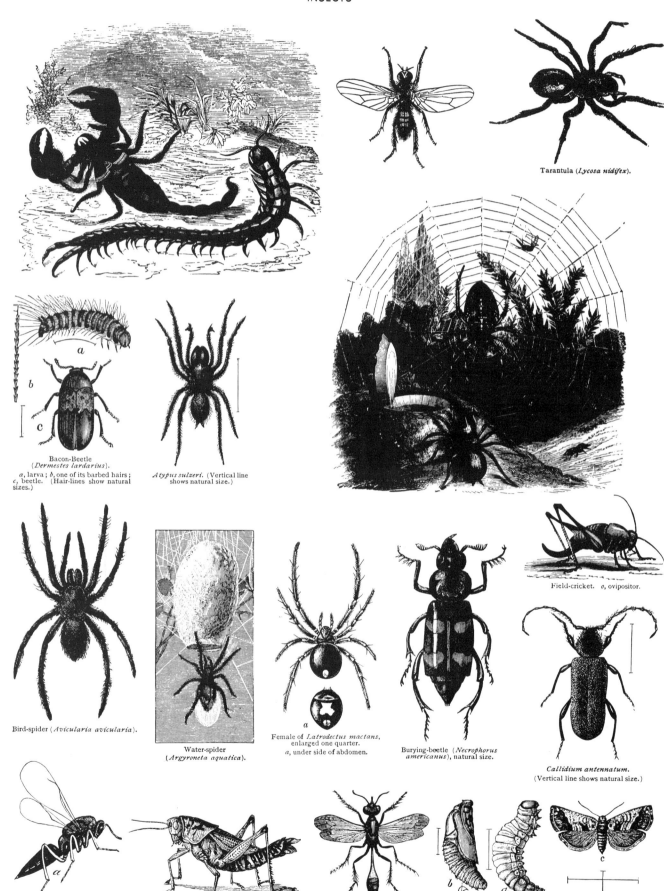

Tarantula (*Lycosa nidifex*).

Bacon-Beetle
(*Dermestes lardarius*).

a, larva; *b*, one of its barbed hairs;
c, beetle. (Hair-lines show natural
sizes.)

Atypus sulzeri. (Vertical line
shows natural size.)

Field-cricket. *o*, ovipositor.

Bird-spider (*Avicularia avicularia*).

Water-spider
(*Argyroneta aquatica*).

Female of *Latrodectus mactans*,
enlarged one quarter.
a, under side of abdomen.

Burying-beetle (*Necrophorus
americanus*), natural size.

Callidium antennatum.
(Vertical line shows natural size.)

a, Abdomen of an Insect (*Iso-
soma hordei*).

Lubber Grasshopper (*Brachystola magna*).

Painted-wing Digger- or Sand-wasp
(*Ammophila pictipennis*), natural
size.

Jumping-seed Carpocapsa (*C. saltitans*).
a, larva; *b*, pupa; *c*, moth. (Cross and perpendicular lines show
natural sizes.)

Gambeson (about 1375). (From Viollet-le-Duc's "Dict. du Mobilier francais.")

Bowman, 15th century. (From Viollet-le-Duc's "Dict. du Mobilier français.")

HENRY V.

Complete Armor, about 1395.

Complete suit of Plate-Armor,

Arbalister. (From Viollet-le-Duc's "Dict. du Mobilier français.")

Ailette with armorial bearings, middle of 13th century. (From Viollet-le-Duc's "Dict. du Mobilier français.")

War-horse Caparisoned, from seal of Philip of Burgundy.

1, Beaver fixed to the corselet: B, vizor; C, beaver. 2, Beaver working on pivots and capable of being raised to cover the face: B, beaver. Both are examples of the middle of the 14th century. (From Viollet-le-Duc's "Dict. du Mobilier français.")

Braconnière (a). (From Viollet-le-Duc's "Dict. du Mobilier français.")

Aigret. (From Hans Burgkmair's "Triumph of Maximilian I.")

Complete Armor of 1195–1205.

Armor and Equipment for man and horse, about 1290.

Helmet with Mesail in two parts.—Spanish, 16th century.

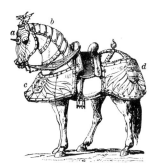

Horse-armor of Maximilian I. of Germany. a, chamfron; b, crinière; c, poitrel; d, croupière, or buttock-piece.

Hauberk, 12th and 13th centuries. (From Viollet-le-Duc's "Dict. du Mobilier français.")

Jack. (From Viollet-le-Duc's "Dict. du Mobilier français.")

Ring-armor. (From Viollet-le-Duc's "Dict. du Mobilier français.")

English Heralds' Tabards of the 17th century. (From a drawing by Van Dyck.)

Steel Armet, about A. D. 1450.

A, Aventaile (def. a). (From Viollet-le-Duc's "Dict. du Mobilier français.")

Armor and Adornments of a Knight equipped for the Tourney. (From Viollet-le-Duc's "Dict. du Mobilier français.")

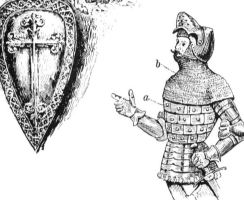

Helmet with Umbrel, 16th century. (From "L'Art pour Tous.")

Armor of Plate. a, plate-armor, as distinguished from b, chain-armor.

ARMOR OF GODFREY OF BOUILLON.

Surcoats. a, 15th century; b, late 13th century. (From Viollet-le-Duc's "Dict. du Mobilier français.")

Pikeman of early 17th century, from print of the time.

Morning-star or War-flail, beginning of 15th century.

NAVAL CROWN.

EARL OF MURRAY'S ARMS. (With bar dexter.)

ARMORIAL ENSIGNS OF SAXONY.

ENGLISH REGALIA.

Addorsed
Affronté
Affronté
Angles
Assis
Gaze
Gemel
Gore
Gules
Gyron

Azure
Bar
Barnacles
Barry
Barry-bendy
Hatchment
Heraldic Knots

Barry-nebuly
Barry-pily
Baton
Bend Sinister
Bendy
Impalement c
Increscent
Indented b
Inescutcheon
Inflamed

Chief Bevel
Bicorporate,
Bordure
Boterol
Caboshed
Interfretted Crescents
Jacent,
Jessant,
Label,
Lattice.

Canton
Checky
Chevron
Chief
Cleché
Lodged
Lozengy
Martlet
Mascle
Naiant

Cockatrice,
Combattant,
Compony,
Conjoined,
Conjoined in Lure,
Or
Orle, 1 a
Pale
Pall, 6 a
Paly of Six, Argent and Gules

Cotised Bend
Couchant Lion,
Counter-changed,
Counter-courant
Counterpaly of Six, argent and azure
Papilloné
Passant
Patonce
Penny-yard Penny
Pheon

Courant
Crescent
Debruised
Displayed,
Dormant,
Pile
Pommettée
Potent
Quartered Arms

Dragon
Embattled Fess
Engouled
Enhanced
Enté en point
Purpure
Quarterly quartered
Raguly
Rampant
Regardant

Erased
Ermine
Escaloped
Escarbuncle
Escutcheon
Rest, 3
Rompu
Sable
Salient
Saltier

Fess
Flanch
Fracted
Fretted
Gardant
Sea Lion
Sejant
Seraph
Spread Eagle c
Statant

99

Tressure Counter-fleury

Vair

Vert

Voided

1   2   3

4   5   6

7   8   9

Weel

Wharrow Spindle

Winnowing Basket

COLORS, OR TINCTURES.

		Gentlemen.	Noblemen.	Princes.
1	Yellow	Or	Topaz	Sol.
2	White	Argent	Pearl	Luna.
3	Red	Gules	Ruby	Mars.
4	Blue	Azure	Sapphire	Jupiter.
5	Black	Sable	Diamond	Saturn.
6	Green	Vert	Emerald	Venus.
7	Purple	Purpure	Amethyst	Mercury.
8	Orange	Tenney	Hyacinth	Dragon's head.
9	Murrey	Sanguine	Sardonyx	Dragon's tail.

HEINRICH VI.

DRAWBRIDGE.

A ROMAN LEGIONARY.

MAXIMILIAN.

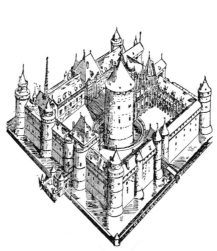

KNIGHT'S COSTUME (1272).

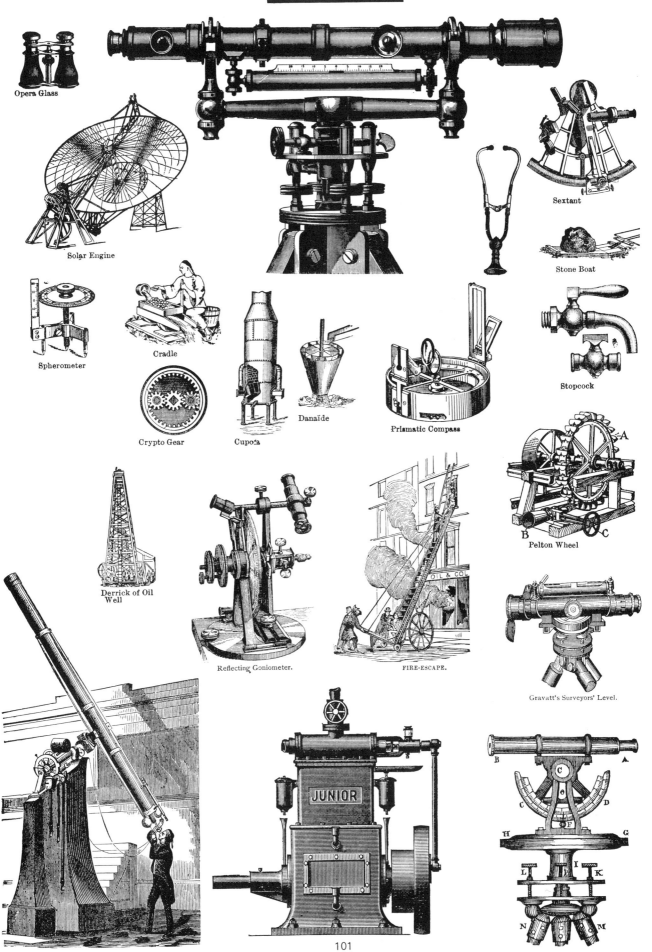

Opera Glass

Solar Engine

Sextant

Stone Boat

Spherometer

Cradle

Crypto Gear

Cupola

Danaïde

Prismatic Compass

Stopcock

Derrick of Oil Well

Reflecting Goniometer.

FIRE-ESCAPE.

OIL & CO

Pelton Wheel

Gravatt's Surveyors' Level.

JUNIOR

TELESCOPE AT CINCINNATI.
(Aperture of object-glass, 12 inches. Total length, 17 feet.)

Blast Furnace

Hand-Goniometer.

Jack-lamp

Armstrong's Hydro-electric Machine.

Winch

Worm Gear

Polariscope

STEAM FIRE-ENGINE.

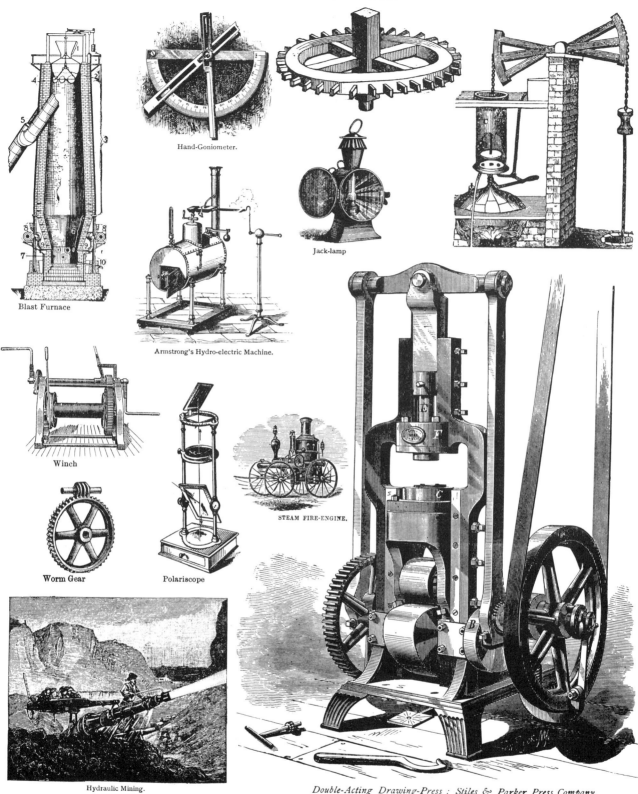

Double-Acting Drawing-Press : Stiles & Parker Press Company.

Hydraulic Mining.

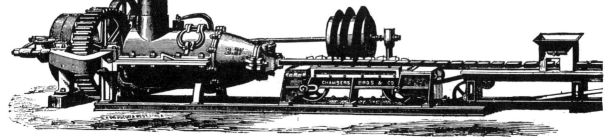

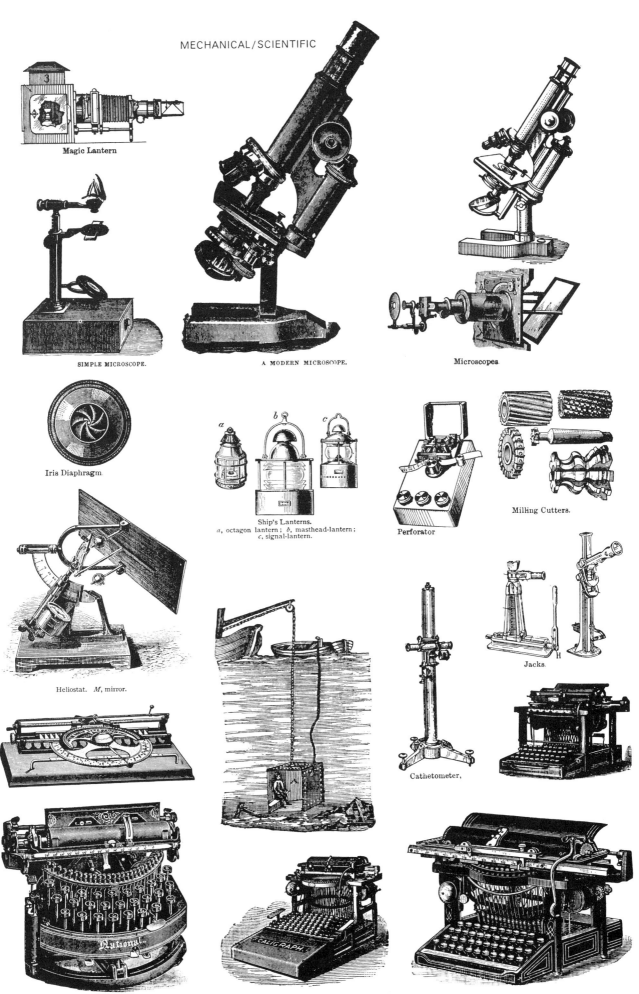

Magic Lantern

SIMPLE MICROSCOPE.

A MODERN MICROSCOPE.

Microscopes.

Iris Diaphragm.

Ship's Lanterns.
a, octagon lantern; b, masthead-lantern;
c, signal-lantern.

Perforator

Milling Cutters.

Heliostat. M, mirror.

Jacks.

Cathetometer.

Knife Switch

Mutoscope

Cramp,

Furnace

Bessemer Process

Copying Press,

Bevel Protractor

Steam Engine, p. 2038.

Counterbalance

Bourdon Gauge

Blocks

COMMON STILL.

Windmills

Forge

Diaphragm Gauge,

Planer Centers.

Band Saw

Still

Chair

Chain Belt

Chain Pump

Check Valve

Siphon

Chain Gear

Panoramic Sight

Seismograph

Change Gear

Chucks

NORMAN BATTLE-AXE.

CATAPULT.

ROMAN WAR-CHARIOT.

BREECH-LOADING CANNON, ON REVOLVING
CARRIAGE; USED BY GUSTAVUS ADOLPHUS
IN SEVENTEENTH CENTURY.

1, a barred helmet; 2, a morion; 3, an open
head-piece; 4, an iron hat or pot.

BATTERING-RAM WITH TOWER.

THE RACK.

King and   Duke and   Baronet and   Esquire or
Prince.   Marquis.   Knight.   Gentleman.

PUCKLE'S MACHINE GUN OF 1718.

MULTIPLE CANNON OF THE SEVENTEENTH CENTURY.

CANNON USED AT THE BATTLE OF CRÉCY, A.D. 1346.

GAUNTLETS.

BREECH-LOADING CANNON OF SIXTEENTH CENTURY —BREECH-
BLOCK SECURED BY A PIN.

ELBOW-SHAPED MORTAR, ABOUT A.D. 1500.

HALBERD.

Hand-grenade of the
15th century. (From
Viollet-le-Duc's "Dict.
du Mobilier français.")

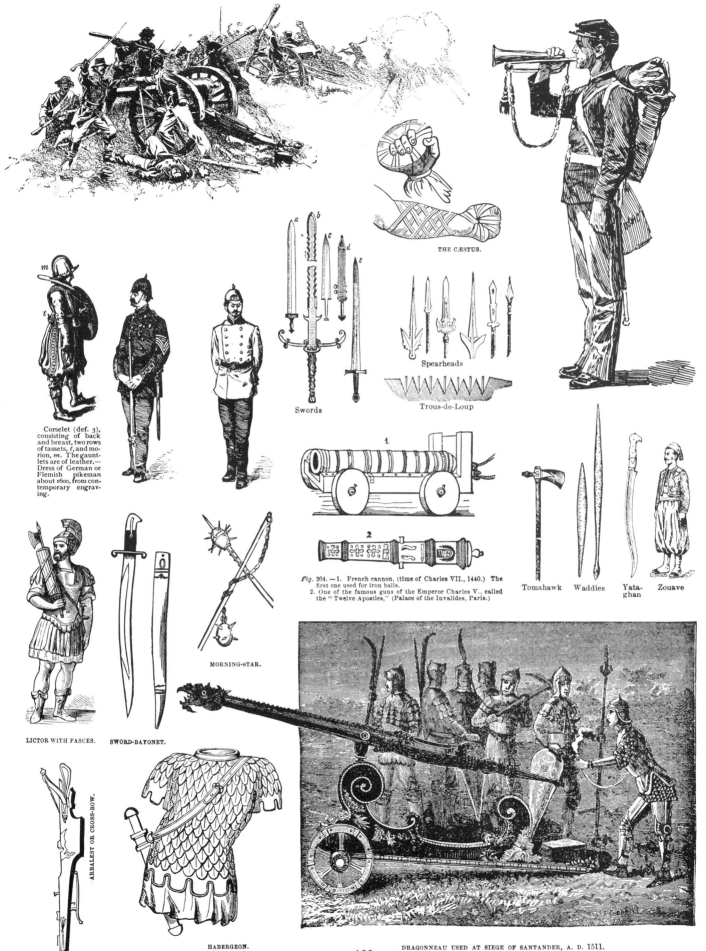

THE CÆSTUS.

Spearheads

Swords

Trous-de-Loup

Corselet (def. 3), consisting of back and breast, two rows of tassets, *t*, and morion, *m*. The gauntlets are of leather.—Dress of German or Flemish pikeman about 1600, from contemporary engraving.

1

2

Fig. 204.—1. French cannon, (time of Charles VII., 1440.) The first one used for iron balls.
2. One of the famous guns of the Emperor Charles V., called the "Twelve Apostles," (Palace of the Invalides, Paris.)

Tomahawk   Waddies   Yata-ghan   Zouave

LICTOR WITH FASCES.

SWORD-BAYONET.

MORNING-STAR.

ARBALEST OR CROSS-BOW.

HABERGEON.

DRAGONNEAU USED AT SIEGE OF SANTANDER, A. D. 1511.

106

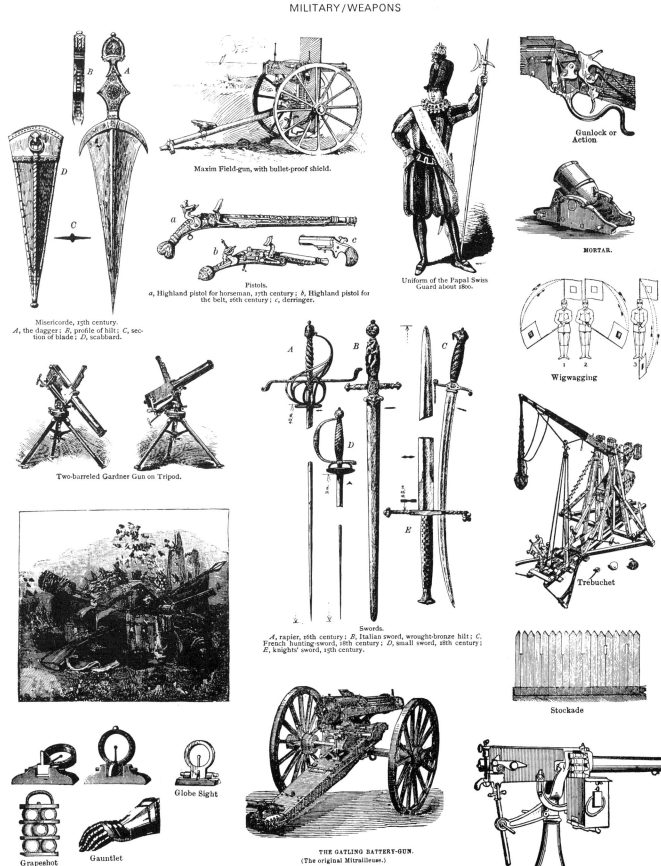

Misericorde, 15th century.
A, the dagger; B, profile of hilt; C, section of blade; D, scabbard.

Maxim Field-gun, with bullet-proof shield.

Pistols.
a, Highland pistol for horseman, 17th century; b, Highland pistol for the belt, 16th century; c, derringer.

Uniform of the Papal Swiss Guard about 1800.

Gunlock or Action

MORTAR.

Wigwagging

Two-barreled Gardner Gun on Tripod.

Swords.
A, rapier, 16th century; B, Italian sword, wrought-bronze hilt; C, French hunting-sword, 18th century; D, small sword, 18th century; E, knights' sword, 15th century.

Trebuchet

Stockade

Grapeshot

Gauntlet

Globe Sight

THE GATLING BATTERY-GUN.
(The original Mitrailleuse.)

MAXIM RAPID-FIRE GUN.
Model of 1897; 1½ inches caliber; naval mounting; fires 300 1-pound shells a minute; velocity, 1,800 feet a second; penetration, 2½ inches of iron.

THE HOWELL TORPEDO.

107

A Member of the Scots Greys, a British cavalry regiment, wearing Sabretash. (After drawing by Elizabeth Butler.)

Military Stock, 18th century.

Carronade.

Bowie-knife and Sheath.

Lyle Life-saving Gun (2.5 inches).

Manton Flint-lock Fowling-piece.
a, hammer; b, flash-pan, or pan; c, touch-hole; d, flint; e, e, cocks.

French Crossbow, 15th century. (From Viollet-le-Duc's "Dict. du Mobilier français.")

Field-gun Carriage.
A, stock. B, cheek. a, lunette; b, trail-plate; c, c, pointing-rings; d, handle; e, e, prolonge-hooks; f, wheel-guard plate; g, lock-chain bolt, nut, and washer; h, turn buckle, chain, and hasp for sponge and rammer; i, stop for rammer-head; k, ear-plate for worm; l, elevating-screw; m, under-strap; n, implement-hook; o, D-ring for hand-spike; q, trunnion-plate; r, cap-square; s, s, cap-square chains and keys; 1, prolonge; 2, sponge and rammer; 3, hand-spike.

Musket-caliber ten-barrel Gatling Gun.

Sword of Miles Standish.

Serpentine. (From an etching by Albert Dürer.)

Crossbow (Arbalist), and Moulinet for bending the bow, 14th and 15th centuries.

a, a', mace of the 13th century; b, mace of the type known as 'holy-water sprinkler' or 'morning-star'; c, mace of the 15th century.

Sword-hilt.

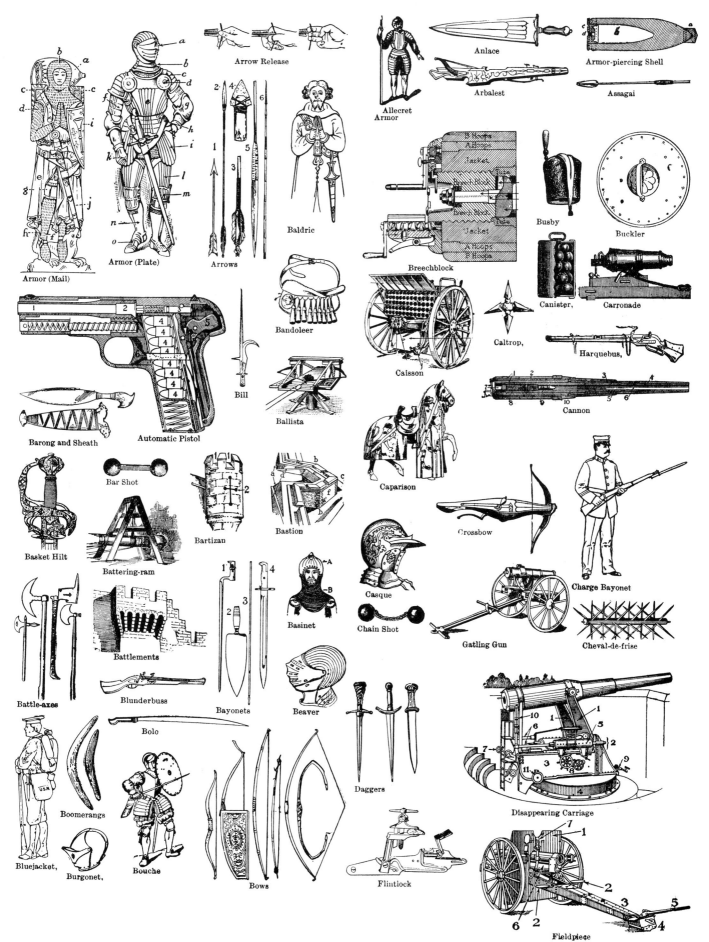

Arrow Release

Anlace

Armor-piercing Shell

Arbalest

Assagai

Allecret Armor

Armor (Plate)

Arrows

Baldric

Busby

Buckler

Breechblock

Canister,

Carronade

Caisson

Caltrop,

Harquebus,

Cannon

Armor (Mail)

Barong and Sheath

Automatic Pistol

Bill

Ballista

Bandoleer

Caparison

Bar Shot

Basket Hilt

Battering-ram

Bartizan

Bastion

Crossbow

Charge Bayonet

Casque

Chain Shot

Battle-axes

Battlements

Blunderbuss

Bayonets

Basinet

Beaver

Gatling Gun

Cheval-de-frise

Bolo

Daggers

Disappearing Carriage

Boomerangs

Bluejacket,

Burgonet,

Bouche

Bows

Flintlock

Fieldpiece

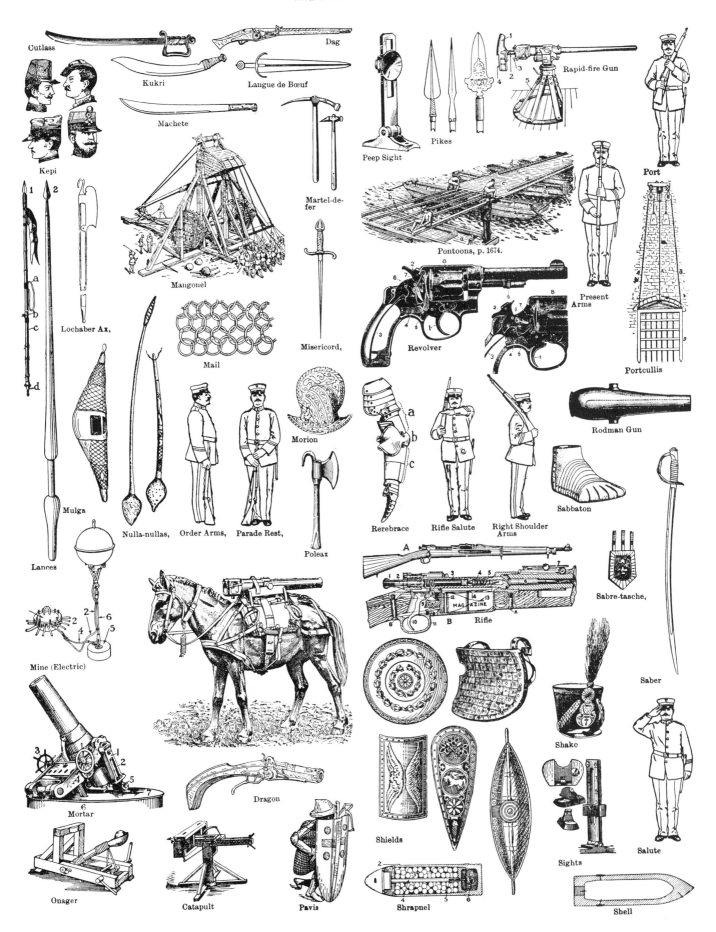

Cutlass

Kukri

Langue de Bœuf

Dag

Machete

Kepi

Lochaber Ax,

Martel-de-fer

Misericord,

Mail

Mulga

Nulla-nullas,

Order Arms,

Parade Rest,

Morion

Poleax

Lances

Mine (Electric)

Mortar

Dragon

Onager

Catapult

Pavis

Shrapnel

Peep Sight

Pikes

Pontoons, p. 1674.

Revolver

Rapid-fire Gun

Port

Present Arms

Portcullis

Rerebrace

Rifle Salute

Right Shoulder Arms

Rodman Gun

Sabbaton

MAGAZINE

Rifle

Sabre-tasche,

Saber

Shields

Shako

Sights

Shell

Salute

(U. S. Army.)

(U. S. Navy.)
Shoulder Straps, p. 1947.

GATLING GUN—NEW NAVY MODEL.

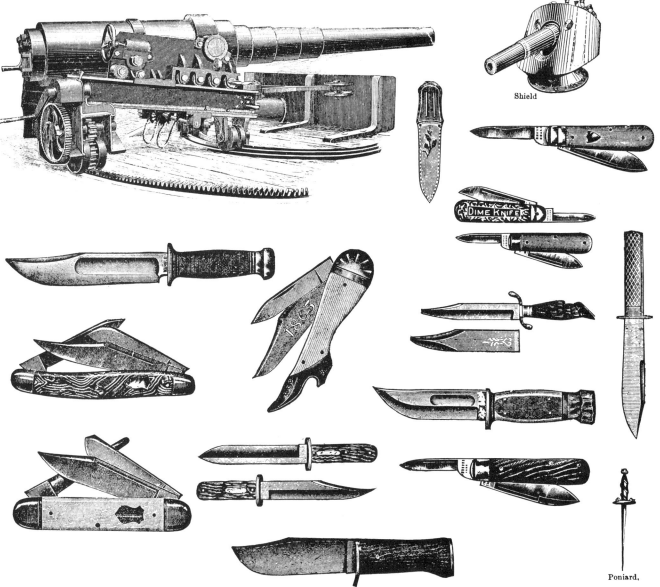

Shield

DIME KNIFE

Poniard,

COLT'S NEW NAVY,
38 & 41 CALIBRE

COLT'S
NEW POCKET
32 CALIBRE.

COLT'S
DOUBLE ACTION,
38 & 41 CALIBRE

COLT SINGLE ACTION ARMY.

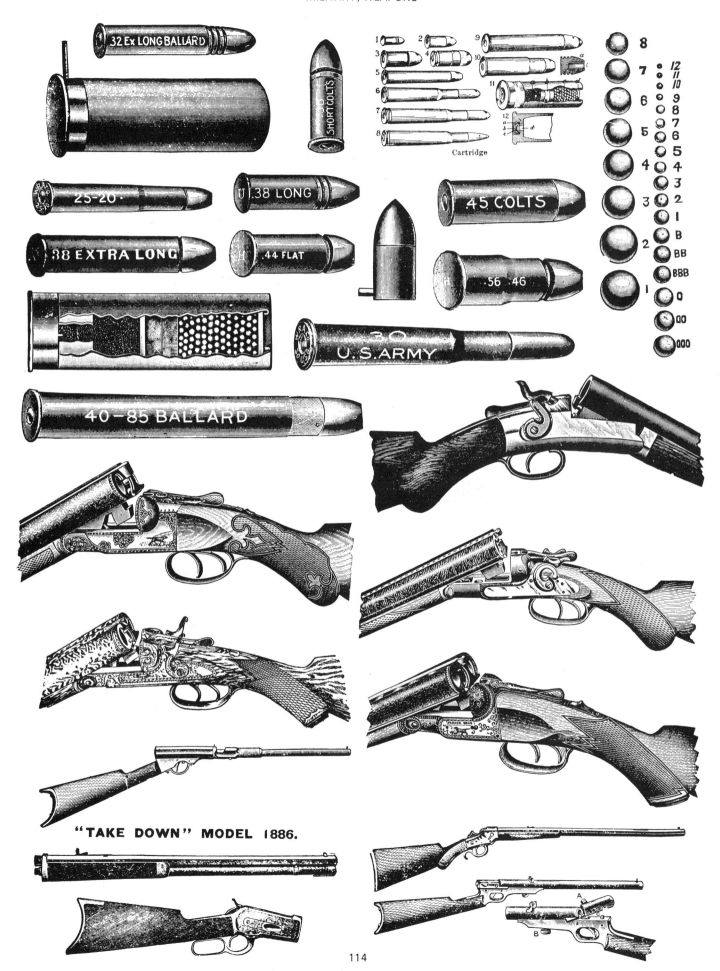

"TAKE DOWN" MODEL 1886.

Obverse.

Obverse.

Reverse.

Britain-crown of James I., British Museum.

Obverse.

Reverse.

Rider of Charles of Egmont, Duke of Gelderland.—British Museum.

Reverse.
Scudo of Pope Gregory XVI.—British
Museum.

Obverse.

Obverse.

Rupee, 1862.—British Museum.

Reverse.

Obverse.

Reverse.
Ruble, 1862.—British Museum.

Obverse.

Reverse.

Salute of Henry VI.—British Museum.

Reverse.
Shilling of Henry VIII.—British Museum.

Obverse.

Bulla of Pope Alexander IV.

Obverse.

Obverse.

Reverse.
Agnel of John II., King of France.

Obverse.   Reverse.
Silver Real of Isabella II.—British
Museum.

Reverse.
Silver Yen.

Reverse.
Unite or Carolus of Charles I., British
Museum.

Obverse.   Reverse.
Gros Tournois of Louis IX., British Museum.

Obverse.

Obverse.
Reverse.
Blanc of Henry VI., British Museum. (Size of the original.)

Obverse.
Reverse.
Blanc of Charles VI. of France, British Museum. (Size of the original.)

Reverse.
Roman As in the British Museum.

Obverse.
Reverse.
Cistophorus of Pergamum, British Museum. (Size of original.)

Obverse.
Reverse.
Bezant (Solidus) of Romanus III.—British Museum. (Size of the original.)

Obverse.

Obverse.
Reverse.
Silver Ambrosino of Milan, British Museum. (Size of the original.)

Obverse.
Reverse.
Carolin of Frederick of Würtemberg, 1810, British Museum. (Size of the original.)

Reverse.
Spur-royal of James I.—British Museum. (Size of the original.)

Allocution.
From an imperial Roman bronze coin in the British Museum.

Accolated Shilling of William III. and Mary. (Size of the original.)

Obverse.
Reverse.
Abbey-counter, in the British Museum.

Obverse.
Reverse.
Bodle of Charles II., British Museum. (Size of the original.)

Obverse.
Reverse.
Augustal, in the British Museum. (Size of the original.)

An ancient Adoration.—Coin of Ephesus struck under Macrinus; British Museum. (Size of the original.)

Obverse of Newark Siege-piece.

Obverse.
Reverse.
Rappen of Billon, 1802; British Museum. (Size of original.)

Obverse.
Reverse.
Aureus of Augustus, British Museum. (Size of the original.)

Chinese Cash of the reign Lung-K'ing (1567-73), the last but four of the Ming dynasty. (Size of the original.)

Obverse.
Reverse.
Argenteus of Caracalla, British Museum. (Size of the original.)

Obverse.
Reverse.
Centime of Napoleon III., British Museum. (Size of the original.)

Obverse.

Obverse. Reverse.
Dime of the United States. (Size of the original.)

Reverse.
Dollar of the United States, 1795. (Size of the original.)

Obverse.

Reverse.
Chaise of Philip VI., British Museum. (Size of the original.)

United States Cent, size of the original.

Obverse.

Reverse.
Broad of James I., British Museum. (Size of the original.)

Obverse. Reverse.
Cardecu (quart d'écu) of Henry IV. of France, in the British Museum. (Size of the original.)

Obverse. Reverse.
Spade-guinea, 1787.— British Museum. (Size of the original.)

Knife-money, two thirds original size.

Obverse. Reverse.
Bawbee of James V.— British Museum. (Size of the original.)

Obverse. Reverse.
Angelot of Henry VI., British Museum. (Size of the original.)

Obverse.

Reverse.
Angel of Edward IV., British Museum. (Size of the original.)

118

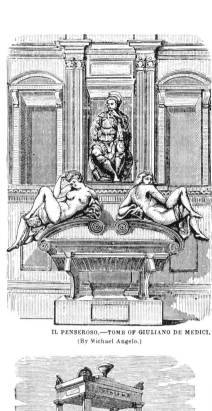

IL PENSEROSO.—TOMB OF GIULIANO DE MEDICI.
(By Michael Angelo.)

FOUNTAIN OF THE PRADO (Madrid).

TOMB OF MOLIÈRE.

TOMB OF NAPOLEON AT THE INVALIDES.

TOMB OF ELIZABETH.
(Westminster Abbey.)

TOMB OF BABER.

Fragment of the Rock at Pilgrim Hall, Plymouth.

SOLDIERS' MONUMENT, GETTYSBURG.

SHRINE,
(From Ely Cathedral, England.)

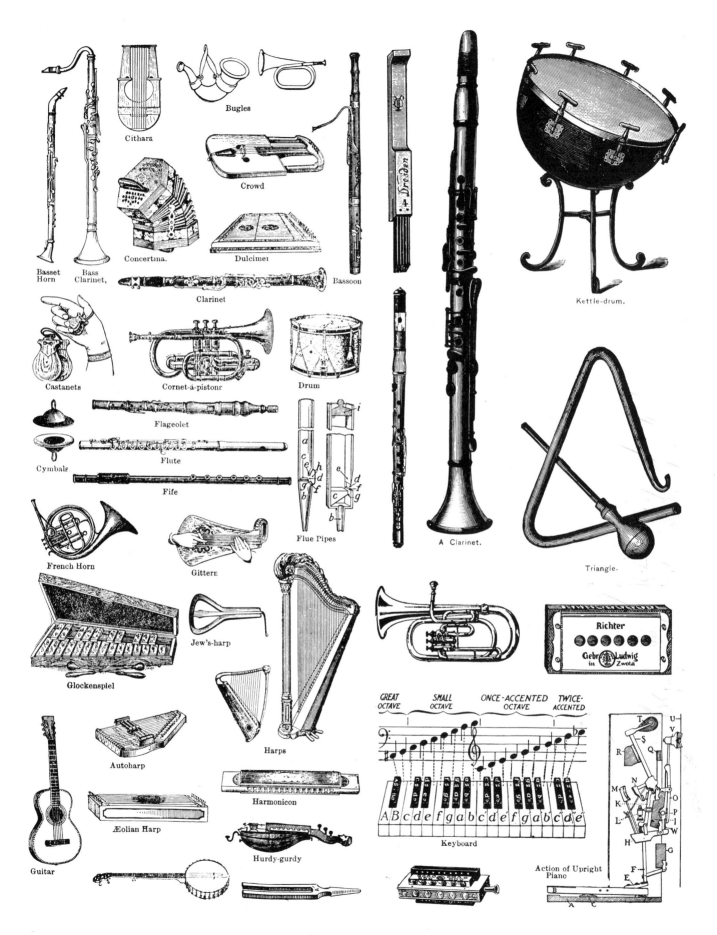

Cithara

Bugles

Crowd

Concertina.

Dulcimer

Basset Horn

Bass Clarinet,

Clarinet

Bassoon

Castanets

Cornet-à-pistons

Drum

Kettle-drum.

Flageolet

Cymbals

Flute

Fife

Flue Pipes

A Clarinet.

Triangle.

French Horn

Gittern

Jew's-harp

Glockenspiel

Harps

Richter

Autoharp

Harmonicon

Æolian Harp

Hurdy-gurdy

Guitar

GREAT OCTAVE   SMALL OCTAVE   ONCE-ACCENTED OCTAVE   TWICE-ACCENTED

A B c d e f g a b c d e f g a b c d e

Keyboard

Action of Upright Piano

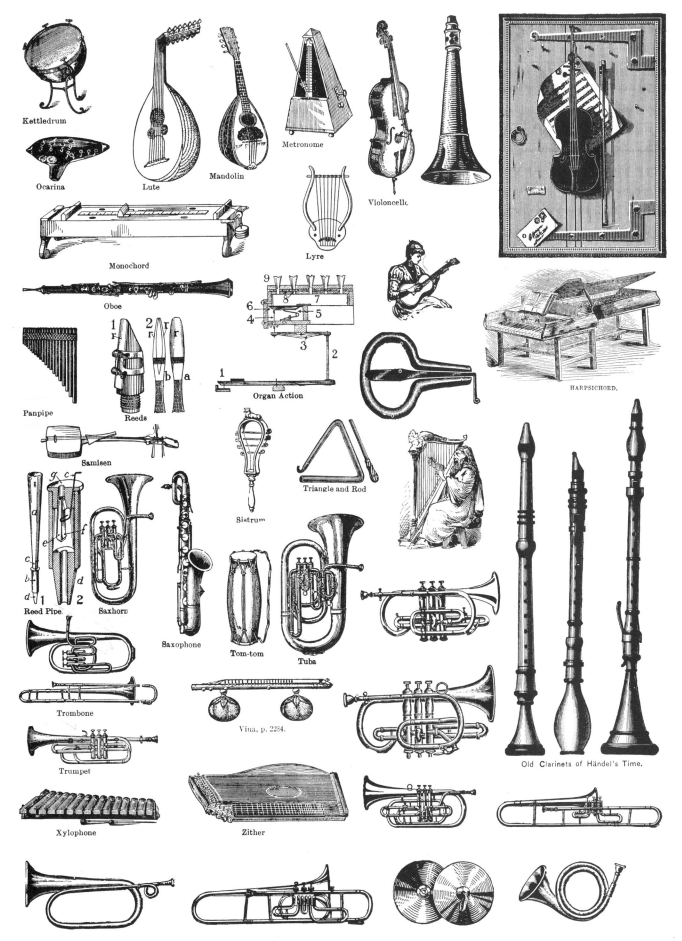

Kettledrum

Ocarina

Lute

Mandolin

Metronome

Violoncello

Monochord

Lyre

HARPSICHORD.

Oboe

Organ Action

Panpipe

Reeds

Samisen

Siatrum

Triangle and Rod

Reed Pipe

Saxhorn

Saxophone

Tom-tom

Tuba

Old Clarinets of Händel's Time.

Trombone

Vina, p. 2284.

Trumpet

Xylophone

Zither

Clarinet, with mouthpiece on a larger scale.

Saxhorn.

French Guitar of the 17th century.

French Harp of the 12th century. (From Viollet-le-Duc's "Dict. du Mobilier francais.")

Mandolin.

The Alto Saxophone.

Double-action Pedal, Concert-Harp.

Mandolin.

Lute.

Viola da Gamba. (From Harl. MS.)

The Viola.

The Oboe.

Old Oboe da Caccia.

Old Oboe d'Amore.

Oboe.

Castagnettes.

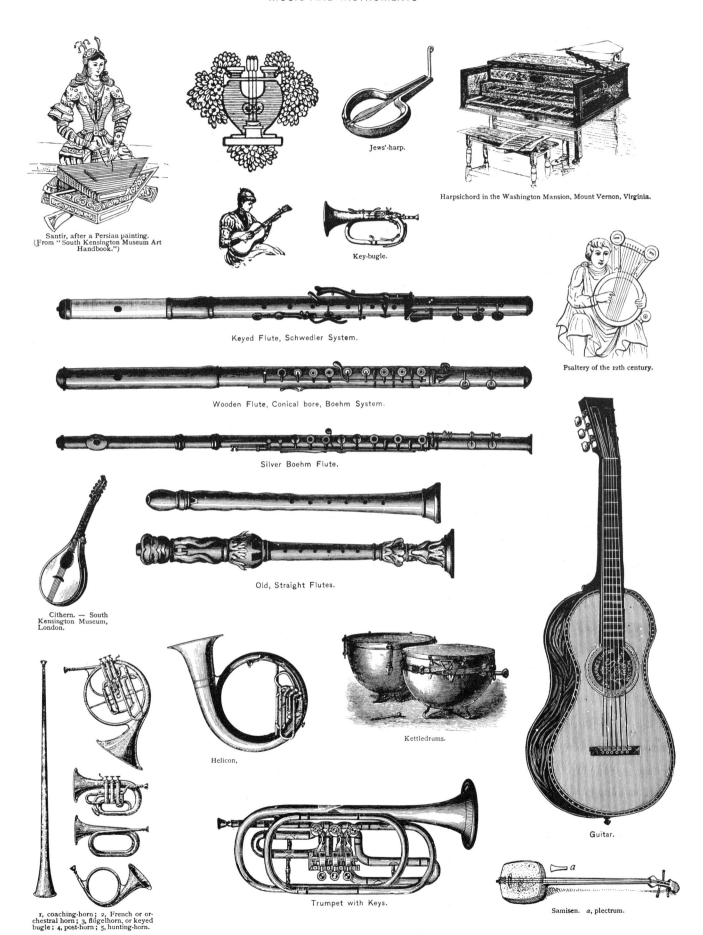

Santir, after a Persian painting.
(From " South Kensington Museum Art
Handbook.")

Jews'-harp.

Key-bugle.

Harpsichord in the Washington Mansion, Mount Vernon, Virginia.

Psaltery of the 12th century.

Keyed Flute, Schwedler System.

Wooden Flute, Conical bore, Boehm System.

Silver Boehm Flute.

Old, Straight Flutes.

Cithern. — South
Kensington Museum,
London.

Helicon,

Kettledrums.

Guitar.

1, coaching-horn; 2, French or or-
chestral horn; 3, flügelhorn, or keyed
bugle; 4, post-horn; 5, hunting-horn.

Trumpet with Keys.

Samisen. a, plectrum.

MUSIC AND INSTRUMENTS

124

Keyboard of a Piano, showing two octaves.

down *up*

Concertinas.

The Violin.

Natural Horn.

Violin.

A, scroll; *B*, pegs; *C*, peg-box; *D*, upper saddle; *E*, finger-board; *F*, sound-holes; *G*, bridge; *H*, tail-piece; *I*, tail-piece ring; *K*, tail-piece button; *M*, neck; *N*, neck-plate; *O*, back; *P*, front or belly; *R*, *R*, bouts; *S*, waist. Inside the violin has six blocks (namely, neck-block, end-pin block, and four corner-blocks), twelve hoop-linings, a bass-bar, and a sound-post.

Old English Bagpipe.

Tuba.

B flat Clarinet.

Saxophone.

Modern Harp.

Cornets-à-Pistons.
1. Ordinary shape. 2. Circular shape.

Bagpipe

Bombardon.

Harpsichord.

Accordion.

Japanese Woman Playing the Koto.

TABOR.

CORNET-À-PISTON.

CASTANET.

The Clariophone.

GRAPHOPHONE

The GRAPHOPHONE

PRUSSIAN PATTERN.

TRITON.

The sun-god Helios rising from the sea, showing radiate head.

A CENTAUR.

NEPTUNE.

HERCULES.

The Triple Hecate. (Relief from Ægina, in collection of Prince Metternich.)

DIANA.
(After an ancient statue.)

The Farnese Hercules.—Statue of the school of Lysippus, in Museo Nazionale, Naples.

JUPITER.

JUPITER OLYMPUS.

Venus and Mercury.

KALI, OR UMA.

A SATYR.

MOLECH, OR MOLOCH.

NISROCH.

THE HINDOO IDOL SULLIAD.

THE IDOL JUGGERNAUT.

Lapith Fighting with Centaur.— Metope of the Parthenon.

Gorgon.— Perseus and Medusa. Archaic
metope from Selinous, Sicily.

MEXICAN IDOL.

DERCETO, OR ATARGATIS.

Winged Genius, from the Harpy Tomb.

Chimera

Dionysus

Faun

Krishna

Laocoön.

Mercury

Diana.

Erinys

Griffin

Fêng-hwang

Osiris

Mænad

Nike.

Gorgoneum, p. 933.

Hathor

Ganesa

Harpy

Hephæstus

Hecate

Mithras

Nergal

Omphalos

Poseidon

Hermes

Hera

Horus

Hershef

Perseus

Parvati

Ptah.

Isis

Indra

Juno

Jupiter

Ker

Quetzalcoatl

Ra.

Satyr

Medusa

129

Giant Geyser, Yellowstone National Park, United States.

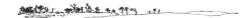

A WATERSPOUT

Nimbus.

Cumulus.

LITTLE STONY FALLS, (60 feet in descent,)
(Little Stony is a tributary of Little Kanawha, or New River, in Giles co.)

CRATER OF THE VOLCANO OF ANTUCO.
(South America.)

THE YOSEMITE VALLEY.

Ship of Fifteenth Century.

STEAM-FRIGATE OF 1850.

COTTON-CHUTE ON THE ALABAMA RIVER.

Chinese Junk.

CHINESE JUNK.

Cadenas of a Duke of Orleans, 15th century. (From Viollet-le-Duc's "Dict. du Mobilier français.")

SQUARE-RIGGED SHIP UNDER FULL SAIL.

Dutch Dogger.

A SPANISH SHIP, (15th cent.)
(From *Epistola Cristoferi Colom.*, &c., 1495.)

THE BAZIN ROLLER-BOAT.

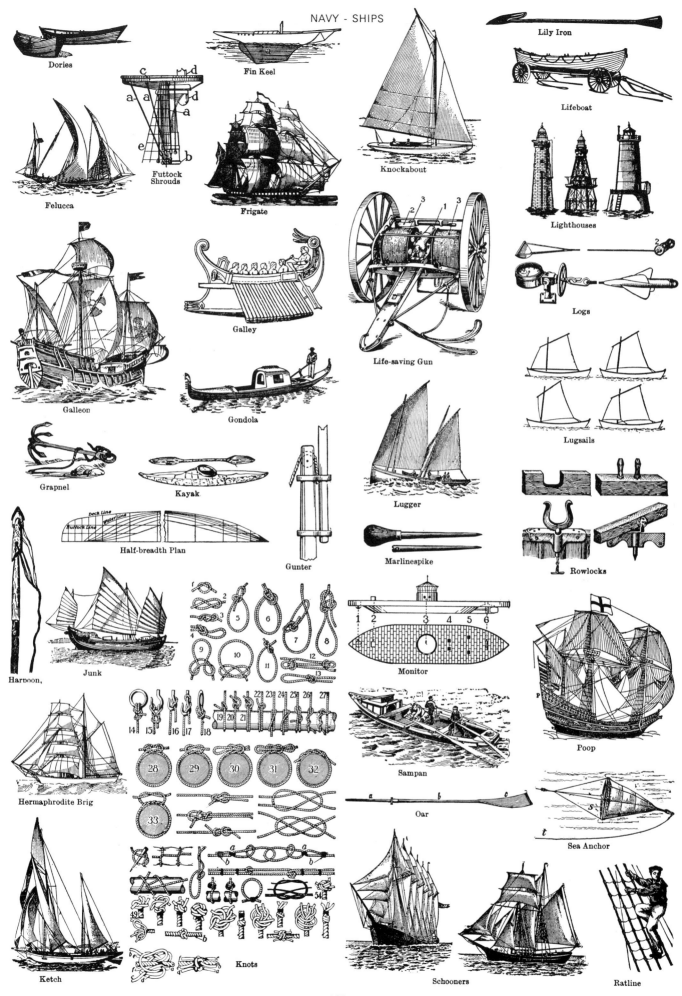

Dories

Fin Keel

Lily Iron

Lifeboat

Futtock Shrouds

Felucca

Knockabout

Frigate

Lighthouses

Logs

Galleon

Galley

Life-saving Gun

Gondola

Lugsails

Grapnel

Kayak

Lugger

Half-breadth Plan

Gunter

Marlinespike

Rowlocks

Harpoon,

Junk

Monitor

Poop

Hermaphrodite Brig

Sampan

Oar

Sea Anchor

Ketch

Knots

Schooners

Ratline

Billyboy.

a, Ringtail, or Studdingsail set upon the Gaff.

Seal Of The Virginia Company.

Figurehead.

Bilander.

Ship's Boat. a a, Rowlocks (notched).

Four-masted Schooner.

1, Bill-board; 2, Bill-port.

Cat-boat.

State Barge.

Race. (Yacht)

Sir Francis Drake's Astrolabe.
Royal Naval College, England.

Proa, with Outrigger.

Dry-dock, or Graving-dock.

A Canton Trading-junk.

Casco of Manila.

Tartan.

Caique.

THE CLERMONT.
(The first steam-packet in the world)

MOBILE.

Schooner.

A CLIPPER SHIP.

Lugger.

Dutch Galiot, with Lee-boards.

Esquimaux Skin-boat.

Lateen Sail.

Caravel, 15th century.

Barkantine.

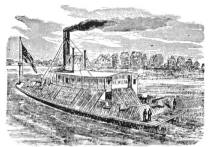

GUNBOAT USED ON THE MISSISSIPPI.

MARINER'S COMPASS.

Ice-boat.

Jangada.

INDIAN CATAMARAN.

1106. — GALLEY.

Fig. 1967. — NORTHMEN'S GALLEY.

A GONDOLA ON THE GREAT LAGOON, (VENICE.)

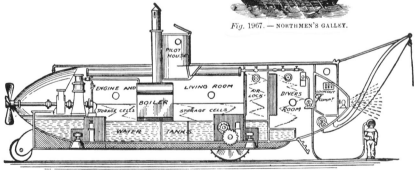

LAKE'S SUBMARINE BOAT "ARGONAUT."

Venetian Gondola.

THE HOLLAND SUBMARINE TORPEDO BOAT.

Ceres.— Wall-painting from Pompeii, Museo Nazionale, Naples.

Priest wearing the Amice. (From a sepulchral brass.)

Barb, middle of 14th century. (From Viollet-le-Duc's "Dict. du Mobilier français.")

Regal. (From an old painting.)

Bipennis. (From a Greek red-figured vase.)

Bourrelet in head-dress of Queen Isabeau of Bavaria; about 1395. (From Viollet-le-Duc's "Dict. du Mobilier français.")

Women's Toques of the 16th century, from portraits of the time. (From "L'Art pour Tous.")

Trunk-hose. 1. Charles IX. of France, 1550-74. 2. Robert Carr, Earl of Somerset (died 1645).

Petticoat-breeches.

1. Doublet, time of Edward IV. 2. Doublet, from portrait of Sir William Russell. 3. Peasecod-bellied Doublet. (Both 2 and 3, time of Elizabeth.) 4. Doublet, time of Charles I.

Ruff.— Close of 16th century.

Bycocket of the 15th century. (From Viollet-le-Duc's "Dict. du Mobilier français.")

Mantle of Man-at-arms, 15th century.

Plume as worn at tourneys and ceremonials, 16th century. (From a print of the time.)

Forms of Hats worn in England in the 16th, 17th, and 18th centuries.

Puffed and Slashed Costume.

Macaroni and Lady in dress of 1770-1775.

Woman wearing a Sack (middle of the 18th century).

Pourpoint, 2.—From a contemporary engraving of Henry II. of France.

Pilgrim, in the recognized dress worn at Rome in the 18th century.

Sir Joshua Reynolds in Domino.—After Thackeray.

Venetian Hose in one piece from waist to feet, 16th century—probably the garment called by foreigners *pantaleone*, or pantaloons.

1, Amice around the neck.
2, Amice worn as a hood.

Mob-cap, 18th century.

British Grenadier of 1745, blowing his fuse to light a grenade.

Highlander wearing modern Kilt and separate Plaid.

Greek Archimandrite.

Torture with the Boot.

Stocks.

Rack.

Biretta.

PEASANTS OF ALICANTE.

EGYPTIAN AND TURKISH SANDALS.

HAIR-DRESS (1782).
(From Stewart's *Whole Art of Hair-dressing*).

STOLA.

MITRE, OR SACRED TURBAN OF THE JEWISH HIGH-PRIEST.

LOUIS XI. AND CHARLES THE BOLD AT PERONNE.

FRENCH COSTUMES, 1793-1797.

A DRUSE GIRL.

DAMASCENE LADY.

COSTUMES OF DALECARLIA, (Sweden.)

BAVARIAN PEASANTS.

COSTUME OF KHOONDOOZ,
(In Independent Tartary, or Turkistan.)

SWEDISH COSTUMES, (Norland.)

HARLEQUIN.

A GENOESE FISHER.

ROMAN EMPEROR

KNIGHT-HOSPITALLER.

A KNIGHT OF THE 15TH CENTURY.
Armed at all points.

James I.

ANCIENT MODE OF BOXING.

LOUIS VII.

Isabella, Queen of Castile.

RODOLPH, COUNT OF HAPSBURG.

COSTUMES, (reign of John.)

JAMES I. OF ENGLAND IN HAWKING COSTUME.
(1603–1625.)

Butterfly Head-dress, middle of 15th century. (From Viollet-le-Duc's "Dict. du Mobilier francais.")

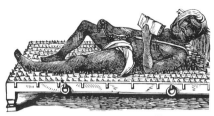

FAKIR ON A BED OF SPIKES. (Kerasis sect.)
(From Gould's *Oriental Drawings*.)

COMMON DRESS OF ASSYRIANS.

A DOMINICAN.
(From Dugdale's *Monasticon*.)

A CHOKEEDAR.
(Village watchman,
Hindostan.)

ASSYRIAN PRIME MINISTER AND ROYAL OVERSEER.

A SULIOT.

LORD HIGH-CHANCELLOR IN HIS STATE ROBES.

HACIENDADO, (Mexican land-owner.)

A WOMAN OF FROSINONE.

NORWEGIAN COSTUMES.

ROMAN WOMAN.

FEMALE INDIAN.

MARKET-WOMEN OF NAPLES.

COSTUME OF LA MANCHA.

A MAÑOLA.

AFGHAN SOLDIER, in winter costu

— AN ALMA.
(Egyptian dancing-girl.)

YOOSOOFZYE.— KINGDOM OF CABOOL.

A WELSH BARD, (11th century.)

POULAINES OR CRACOWS.

A DOGE OF VENICE.

EGYPTIAN MUMMY.

COSTUMES, (end of the 17th century.)

COSSACK OF THE DON.

GIRL OF BAGDAD.

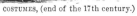

A NOBLE OF COCHIN CHINA.

CAUCASIAN TYPE.

NADIR SHAH, (king of Persia.)
(From Fraser's Hist. of "Nadir Shah.")

1. Kee Wongee, or prime minister.   2. A trooper.

JAPANESE WOMEN: MOTHER, DAUGHTER, AND
SERVANT.

KUNG-FU-TSE, (*Confucius*.)
(Traditional likeness.)

Tee Yee Neen Ho Ga Ron Emperour of the Six Nacions

A NOBLEMAN AND A BUDDHIST PRIEST.

MANTCHOO SOLDIERS.

THE GRAND LAMA, OR DALAI-LAMA.

154

PEASANT OF ORIHUELA.

A COUNTRYWOMAN.

FILIGREE ORNAMENT.
(From a drawing by M. Mariana, in the
Florence exhibition, 1861.)

URDHABAHUS, or OODOOBAHOOS.
(From "Les Hindous," by Solvyn.)

DANCING DERVISHES.

A MODERN GREEK GIRL.

A LAPLANDER.

A JEWISH LADY.

WINDSOR HERALD.

FEMALE ICELANDER.

GREEK PRIEST RECEIVING A CONFESSION.

EGYPTIAN GIRL.

COSTUME OF SZEKLERS, (Transylvania.)

Queen Elizabeth.

LADY OF THE COURT OF QUEEN CATHERINE DE MEDICI

LOUIS XIV.

A MACARONI.

MOLDAVIAN COUNTRY-WOMAN.

ENGLISH ARQUEBUSIER.

Full-length portrait of Dr. Johnson, in the dress worn by him in his journey to the Hebrides.

FRENCH COSTUMES, 1770.

COSTUMES OF THE TIME OF EDWARD III.

DOUBLET.

DRINKING WASSAIL.

HEAVY-ARMED GREEK WARRIOR.

FEMALE COSTUMES, (time of Edward I.)

General John Stark

A CAVALIER AND LADY.
(Time of Charles I.)

General Charles Lee

Eon OhKoan King of the River Nation

WATER-CARRIER. (Chili.)

WINTER VILLAGE OF ESQUIMAUX.

Bolzius.

ESQUIMAU.

MATTHIAS.

KARL IV.

MAXIMILIAN II.

LEOPOLD II.

WOMAN OF TRAPANI.

A SLOVAK.

LEOPOLD I.

MORAVIAN COUNTRY-WOMAN.

SERB WOMAN.

Gorgets.

1, Hausse-col (*a*) attached to the brigandine, 15th century. 2, Hausse-col (*a*) worn over mail, early 15th century. (From Viollet-le-Duc's " Dict. du Mobilier français.")

INDIAN OF PARAGUAY.

GIRL IN DANCING DRESS.

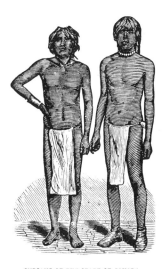

INDIANS OF THE STATE OF SONORA.

BETSIMASARAKA WOMAN AND CHILD.

MALAYS OF BORNEO.

TATTOOED CHIEFS OF THE MARQUESAS ISLES.

AN AMAZON.

YOUNG HOTTENTOT.

Mandan Indian.

Lord and Lady of Secotan.

NUBIAN GIRL.

HEAD-DRESSES, AND FASHION OF WEARING PATCHES.
(From a French drawing, 1739.)

George III.

John Smith.

Sir Walter Raleigh.

FRANÇOIS, DUKE DE GUISE (1550).

COSTUME OF FRANCIS II.
(France.)

ENGLISH DUKE, IN HIS STATE ROBES.

Coat of Mail, western Europe;
13th century. (From Viollet-le-
Duc's "Dict. du Mobilier français.")

A SAXON SOLDIER.

GEOFFREY PLANTAGENET.

COSTUME OF THE TIME OF ELIZABETH, (1575.)

HIGH-PRIEST.

OSCEOLA.

THE NORTH-AMERICAN INDIAN.

VIEW OF THE RANGE OF THE VENTANA, AND
HUILLICHES INDIANS.

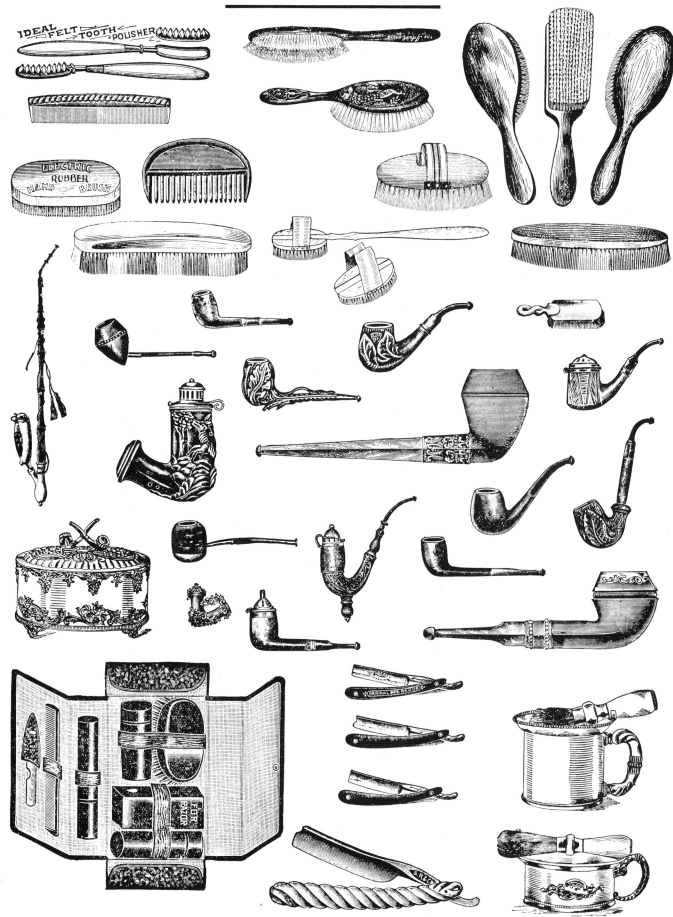

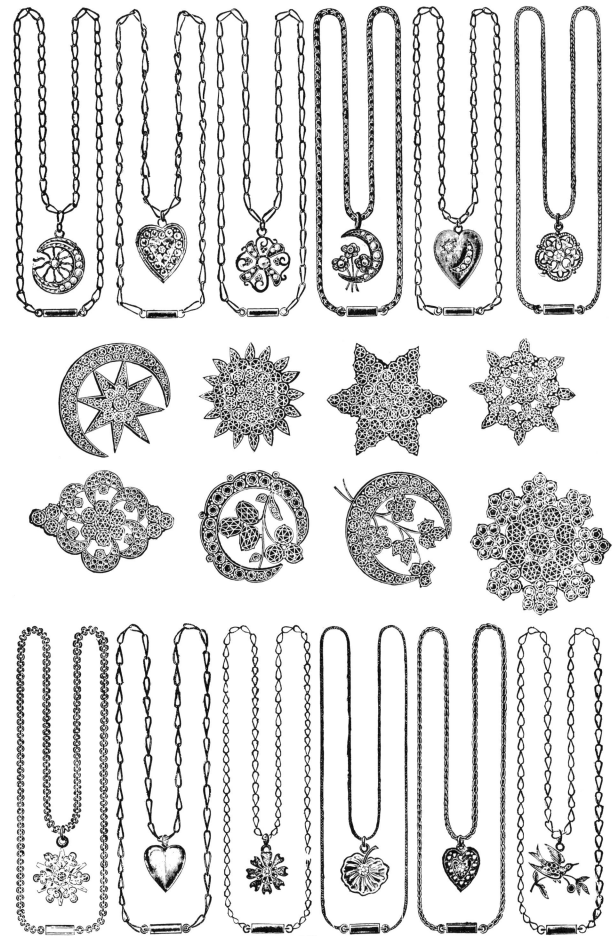

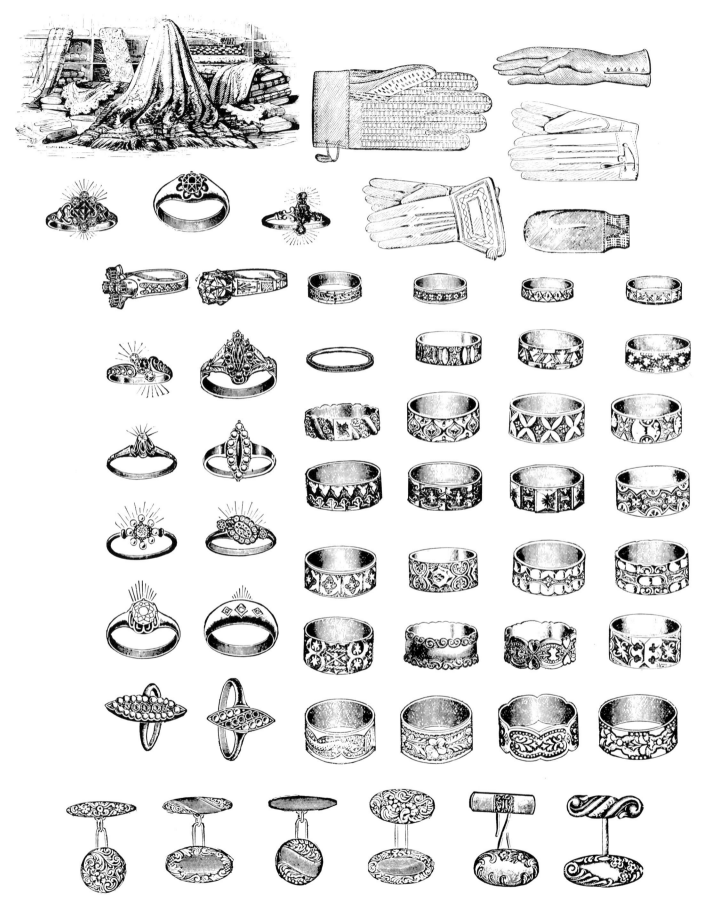

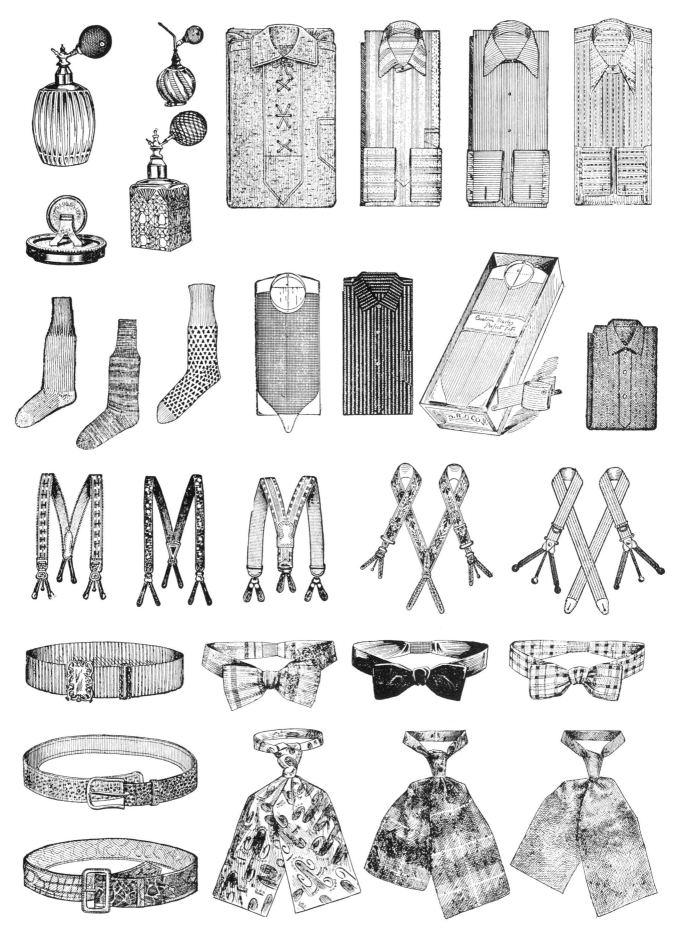

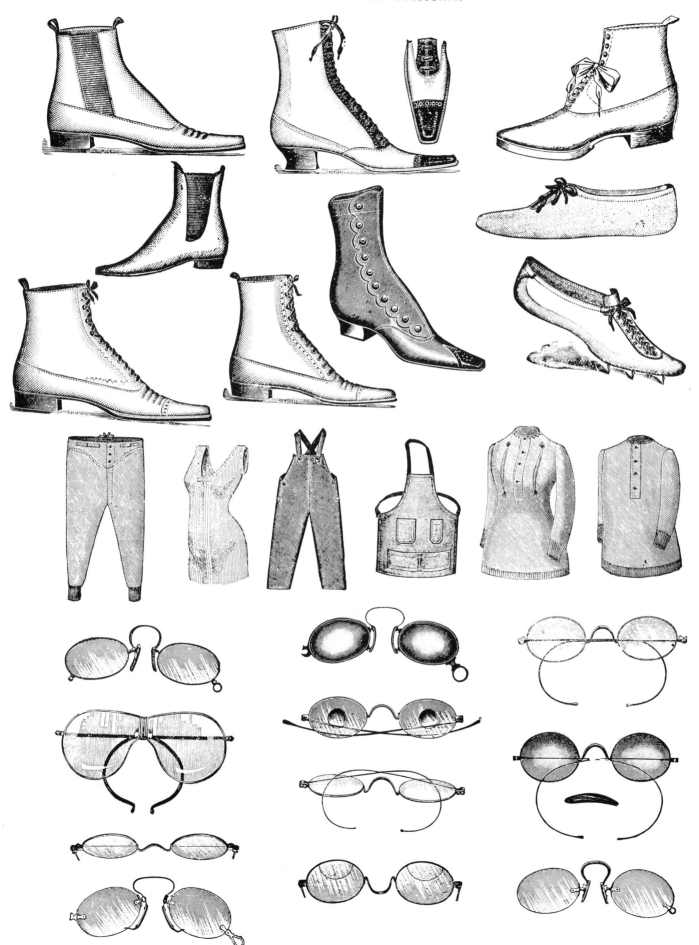

Aspergillum

Bands

Cardinal's Hat

Chalice

Alb

Biretta

Chasuble

Crosier

Ciborium,

Font

Cruet

Lama with Prayer Wheel,

Gonfalon

Lectern,

Hearse

Monstrance,

Phylacteries,

Mantelletta

Miter

Pax

Pyx

Pulpit of Church of Santa Maria Novella, Florence

Stalls in Santa Maria Gloriosa dei Frari, Venice

Stoup

Tiara

XP

Silver Chef in the cathedral of Florence, containing part of the skull of Saint Zenobius. By Andrea di Ardito, 1330.

Chrismatory

Pastoral Crook

PASTORAL STAFF.

Necklace, Tortoise-Shell

Detail from apse of the Basilica of Torcello, near Venice; 12th century.

THE LAST SUPPER, BY RAPHAEL. A FRESCO IN THE REFECTORY OF THE FORMER CONVENT OF SAN ONOFRIO, FLORENCE.

CROSS OF THE 10TH CENTURY, AT MONASTER-BOICE, IRELAND.

Abat-voix, pulpit of Trinity Church, New York.

Bronze Crucifix.—Romanesque style, decorated with enamels.

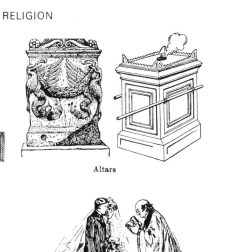

Altars

Allegory – The Church. Cathedral of Worms, 13th century. The beast with four heads symbolizes the Four Gospels. (Viollet-le-Duc's "Dict. de l'Architecture.")

Agnus Dei

Censer

Wimple, from a statue of Jeanne d'Evreux, Queen of France, consort of Charles IV. The statue probably dates from about 1327. (From Viollet-le-Duc's "Dict. du Mobilier français.")

Trinity, late 13th century.— Church of St. Urbain, Troyes, France. (From Viollet-le-Duc's "Dict. de l'Architecture.")

The Nimbus as variously represented in Sacred and Legendary Art. —1, God the Father; 2 and 3, Christ; 4, Charlemagne; 5, Emperor Henry II.

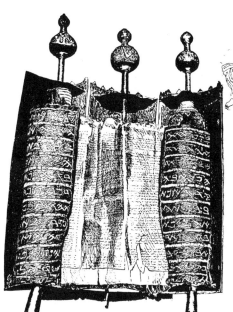

Quadra.—"Annunciation," by Luca della Robbia, in the Borgo San Jacopo, Florence.

Volume of the ancient type. Pentateuch of the Samaritans, used in their Synagogue at Shechem.

Faldstool

Mandorla.—From Assumption of the Madonna, by Orcagna; Church of Or San Michele, Florence.

Glory.—Figure of Christ, façade of Cathedral of Angoulême, France; 12th century.

Copes.

Personification.—The "Church of Christ," from the west front of the Cathedral of Notre Dame, Paris (13th century sculpture).

Brass of Eleanor Bohun (died 1399), in Westminster Abbey.

Aureola.—Figure of Christ, from tympanum of portal of St. Trophime, Arles, France; 12th century.

Bambino, Church of Ara Cœli, Rome.

The Victory of Samothrace, in the Louvre Museum.

Centaur.— Museo Capitolino, Rome.

Ionian Chiton.—Tanagra figurine, Berlin Museum.

Monumental Cross, Eyam, Derby-
shire, England.

Figure in the Round.
The Sleeping Ariadne, in the Vatican Museum.

Bust of Homer, Museo Nazionale, Naples.

Mercury.— Statue of Greek
workmanship, in the British
Museum, London.

Hellenistic Sculpture.—The Apollo Belvedere, Vatican Museum, Rome.

1   2
1. The Venus of Medici, in the Uffizi Gallery, Florence.
2. The Venus of Melos, in the Louvre Museum.

Athene.—The Minerva Farnese, Museo Nazionale, Naples.

Clio.— Statue in the Vatican, Rome.

Archaistic Bronze
Statuette from Verona,
in the British Museum,
in imitation of Greek
work of the sixth cen-
tury B. C.

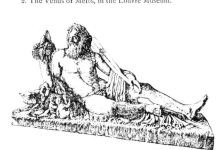

River-god.— Tiberis, the River Tiber, in the Louvre Museum.

Promachos.—Athene the De-
fender. (Marble from Herculane-
um, in the Museo Nazionale, Naples.)

Renaissance Sculpture.—The "David" of Michelangelo, in the Accademia, Florence, Italy.

Torso Belvedere, showing "checker-board" appearance.

Androsphinx of Thothmes III. (15th century B. C.), Boulak Museum, Cairo.

Roman Toga.—Statue of the Emperor Tiberius.

Rhodian School of Sculpture.—The Laocoön, in the Vatican. (The existing incorrect restorations of arms, etc., are omitted.)

Hollow-relief or Cavo-rilievo Sculpture.—Court of Edfu, Egypt; Ptolemaic age, 2d century B. C.

Bracæ.—Statue of Paris, Vatican Museum.

Sphinx.—Greek sculpture in the British Museum.

Caryatids.
Porch of the Erechtheum at Athens.

Satyr.—The Barberini Faun, at Munich.

Amazon.
Statue in the Vatican, perhaps a copy of the type of Phidias.

Hera Ludovisi, wearing Stephane.

Roman Art.— Bust of the Empress Faustina, wife of Antoninus Pius.

Doryphorus.— Copy after Polycletus, Museo Nazionale, Naples.

Discobolus.— Vatican Museum, Rome.

Egyptian Sculpture.
General Rahotep (Rahotpou) and his Wife, Princess Nefert (Nofrit), period of the first Theban empire.

Sculptured Stele.— Monument of the Knight Dexileos (who fell before Corinth 394 B. C.), on the Sacred Way, Athens.

Aphrodite.
Copy of the Cnidian Statue by Praxiteles, Vatican Museum.

Artemis (Diana) the Huntress.— Louvre Museum.

Ægis.— Varvakeion Statuette of Athena.

Ares.— Statue in the Villa Ludovisi, Rome.

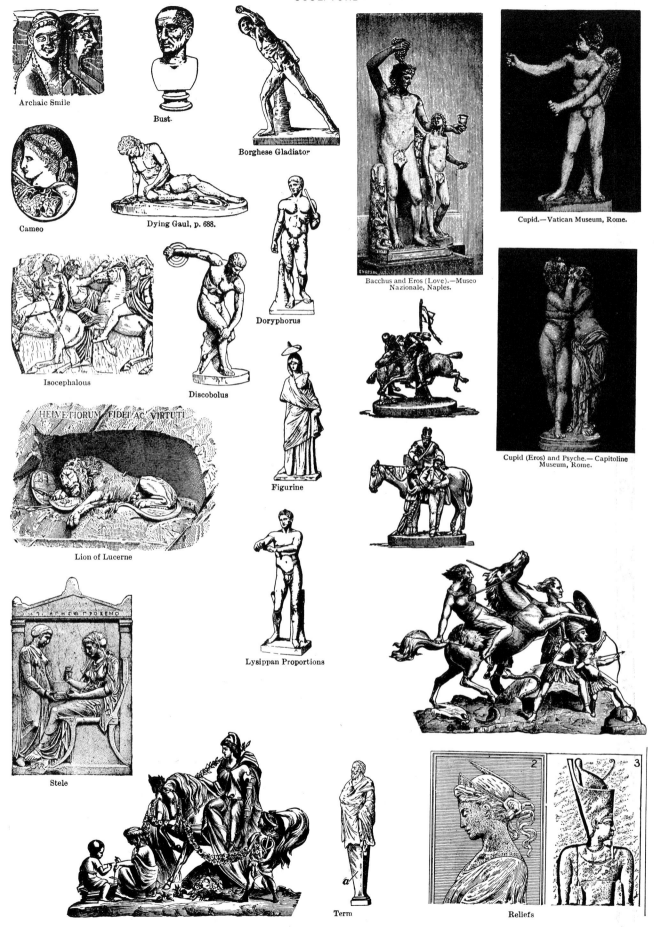

Archaic Smile

Bust.

Borghese Gladiator

Cameo

Dying Gaul, p. 688.

Doryphorus

Cupid.—Vatican Museum, Rome.

Bacchus and Eros (Love).—Museo Nazionale, Naples.

Isocephalous

Discobolus

Figurine

Cupid (Eros) and Psyche.—Capitoline Museum, Rome.

HELVETIORUM FIDEI AC VIRTUTI

Lion of Lucerne

Lysippan Proportions

Stele

Term

Reliefs

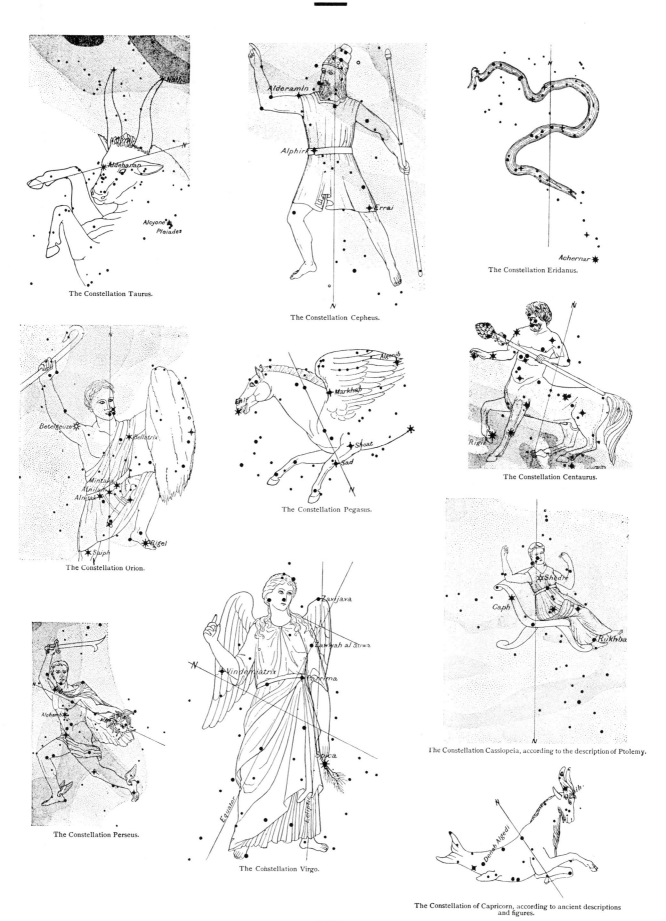

The Constellation Taurus.

The Constellation Cepheus.

The Constellation Eridanus.

The Constellation Orion.

The Constellation Pegasus.

The Constellation Centaurus.

The Constellation Perseus.

The Constellation Virgo.

The Constellation Cassiopeia, according to the description of Ptolemy.

The Constellation of Capricorn, according to ancient descriptions and figures.

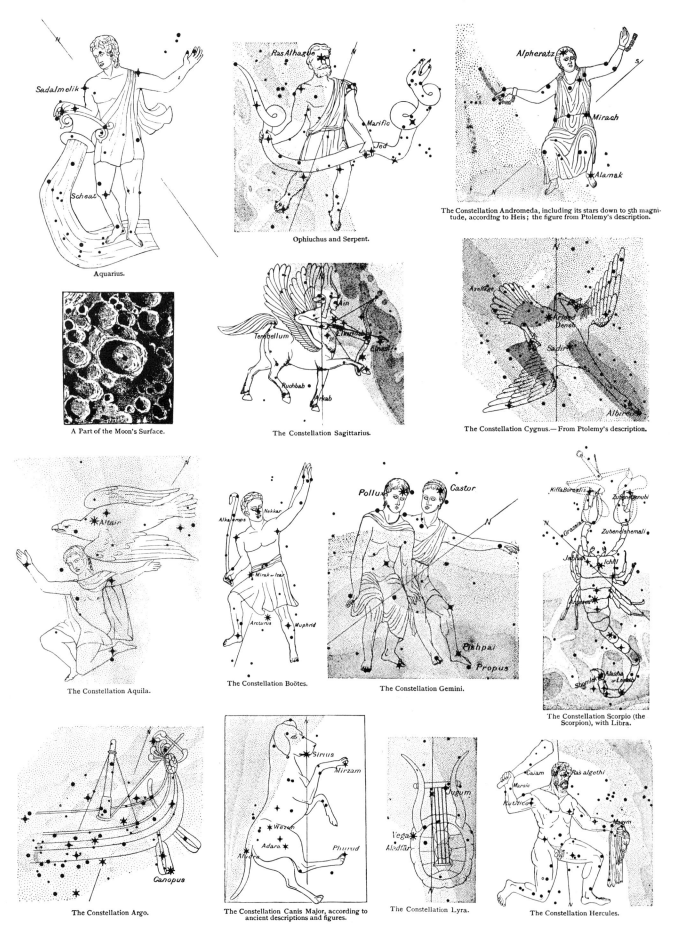

Aquarius.

Ophiuchus and Serpent.

The Constellation Andromeda, including its stars down to 5th magnitude, according to Heis; the figure from Ptolemy's description.

A Part of the Moon's Surface.

The Constellation Sagittarius.

The Constellation Cygnus.— From Ptolemy's description.

The Constellation Aquila.

The Constellation Boötes.

The Constellation Gemini.

The Constellation Scorpio (the Scorpion), with Libra.

The Constellation Argo.

The Constellation Canis Major, according to ancient descriptions and figures.

The Constellation Lyra.

The Constellation Hercules.

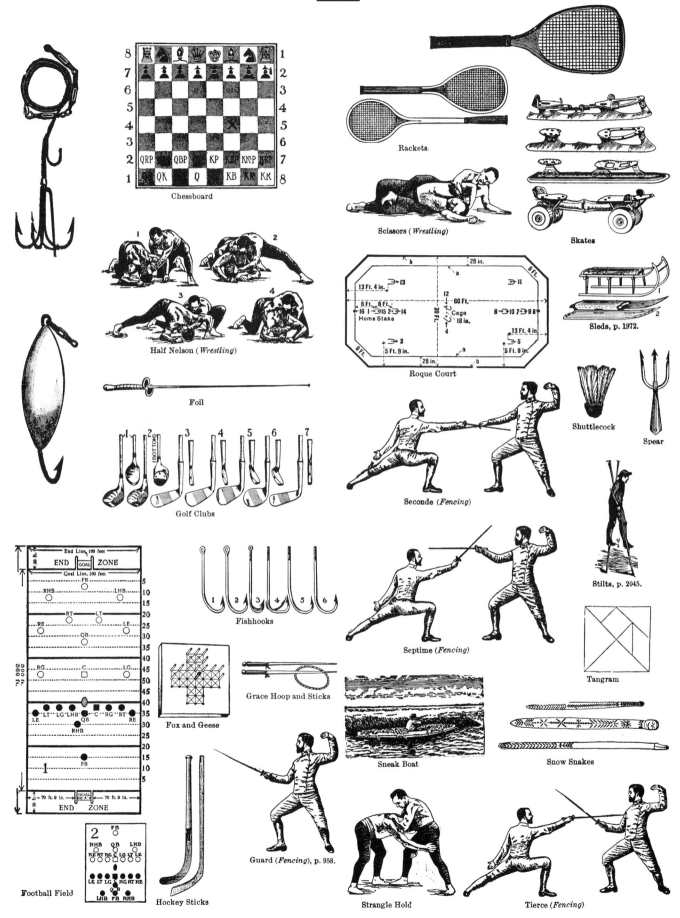

Chessboard

Rackets.

Scissors (*Wrestling*)

Skates

Half Nelson (*Wrestling*)

Roque Court

Sleds, p. 1972.

Foil

Shuttlecock

Spear

Golf Clubs

Seconde (*Fencing*)

Stilts, p. 2045.

Fishhooks

Septime (*Fencing*)

Tangram

Fox and Geese

Grace Hoop and Sticks

Sneak Boat

Snow Snakes

Guard (*Fencing*), p. 958.

Football Field

Hockey Sticks

Strangle Hold

Tierce (*Fencing*)

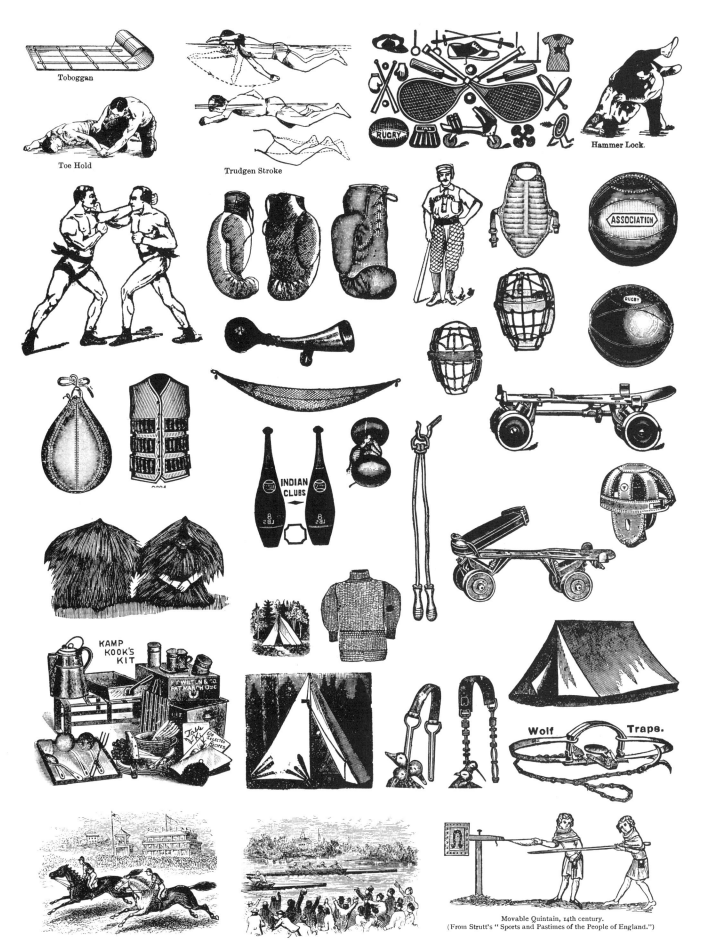

Toboggan

Toe Hold

Trudgen Stroke

Hammer Lock.

ASSOCIATION

RUGBY

INDIAN CLUBS

KAMP KOOK'S KIT

Wolf Traps.

Movable Quintain, 14th century.
(From Strutt's " Sports and Pastimes of the People of England.")

S. R. & Co.
850
SOLDER
SOLDER IRON
HEEL PLATES
WRENCH
BRISTLES
NEEDLE
WAX
ROSIN
COPPER RIVETS
HALF SOLING NAILS
HALF SOLING TACKS
HEEL NAILS
RUBBER CEMENT
SOLDERING FLUID
LEATHER CEMENT
SHOE PEGS-BEST QUALITY
PUNCH

AX STONE

NO. 115

VULCAN ANVIL

Band-saw.

Redlich's warranted FAUCETS

TOOLS

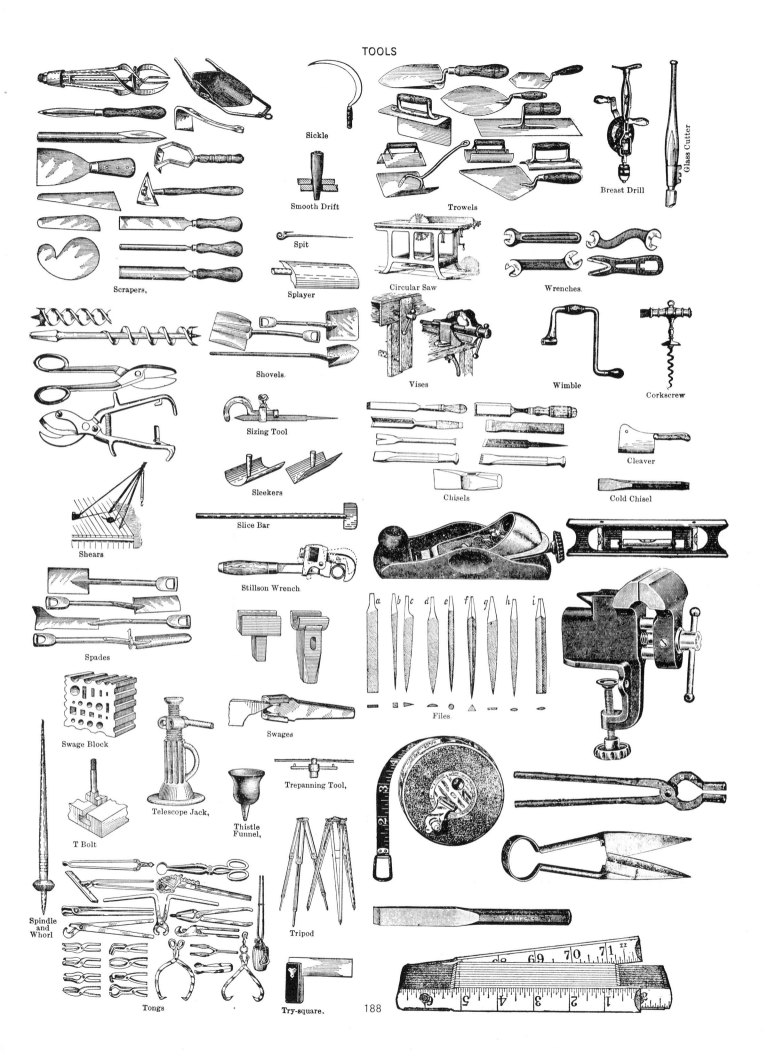

Sickle

Smooth Drift

Scrapers,

Spit

Splayer

Trowels

Breast Drill

Glass Cutter

Circular Saw

Wrenches.

Shovels.

Vises

Wimble

Corkscrew

Sizing Tool

Chisels

Cleaver

Sleekers

Cold Chisel

Slice Bar

Shears

Stillson Wrench.

Spades

Files.

Swage Block

Swages

Trepanning Tool,

T Bolt

Telescope Jack,

Thistle Funnel,

Spindle and Whorl

Tripod

Tongs

Try-square.

RUSSIAN SLEDGE.

MODE OF TRAVELLING IN MAURITIUS.

TREVITHICK AND VIVIAN STEAM CARRIAGE.
CONSTRUCTED IN 1801.

BOKHARIAN LADIES TRAVELLING.

ELEPHANT WITH HOWDAH.
(From Major Luard's "Views in India.")

SIX-WHEEL ELECTRIC MINE LOCOMOTIVE.

EXPRESS PASSENGER LOCOMOTIVE, GREAT NORTHERN RAILWAY, ENGLAND.

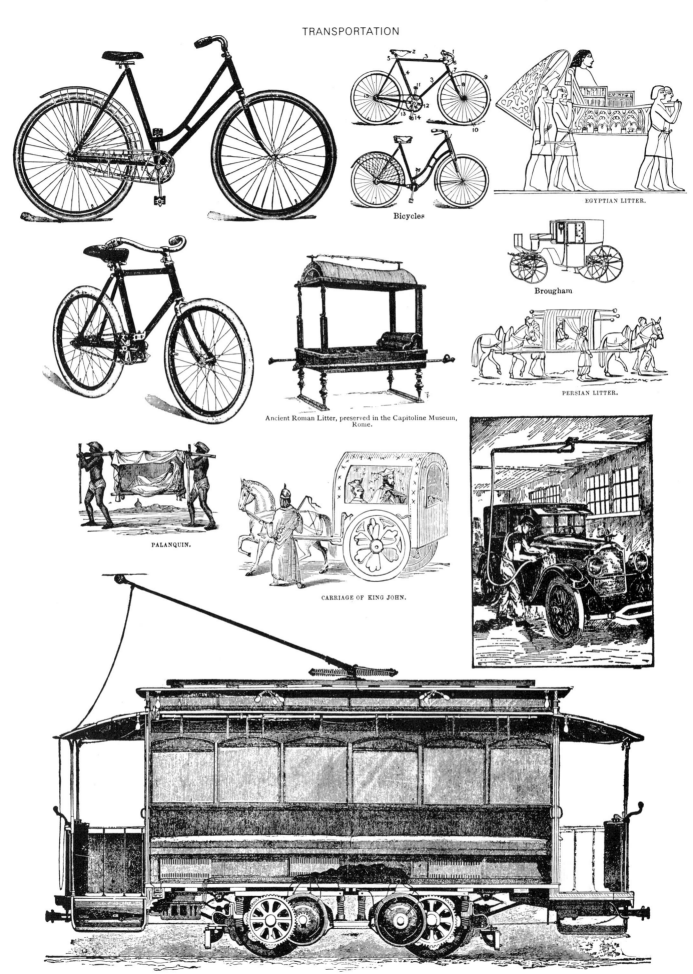

Bicycles

EGYPTIAN LITTER.

Brougham

Ancient Roman Litter, preserved in the Capitoline Museum, Rome.

PERSIAN LITTER.

PALANQUIN.

CARRIAGE OF KING JOHN.

TROLLEY CAR AND ITS ELECTRICAL CONNECTIONS.

Calèche

Chaise

Clarence

Rockaway

Road Cart

Sleigh

Carromata

Chariotee

Coupé

Running Gear

Sedan

Coach

Concord Buggy

Stanhope

Telega

Dogcart

Dray

Surrey

Victoria

Dump Cart

Gig

Tricycles

Buckboard

Palanquin

Hansom

Wagonette

Phaëton

Jinrikisha

Landau

Buggy

Motor Cycle

Bobsled

EIGHT-WHEEL EXPRESS ELECTRIC LOCOMOTIVE.

Calash

Traveling-sledge of Peter the Great.

Hackery.

THE FILS DE PEUGEOT FRERES CARRIAGE—PETROLEUM MOTOR. WINNER OF THE ROAD RACE FROM
PARIS TO BORDEAUX AND RETURN.

STATE-COACH OF QUEEN ELIZABETH.

Polyanthus Narcissus (Narcissus Tazetta).

Flowering Plant of *Matricaria inodora.*
a, ray-flower; *b*, disk-flower; *c*, achenium.

Bedegars.

Rock-rose (*Cistus Creticus*).

Black Mulberry (*Morus nigra*).

The Ramie-plant (*Bœhmeria nivea*).

Branch of Beam-tree (*Pyrus Aria*).

Orchid (*Cattleya citrina*).

Cycas circinalis.
From Le Maout and Decaisne's " Traité général de Botanique.")

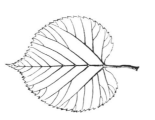

Dogwood (*Cornus florida*).

Baobab of Madagascar (*Adansonia Madagascariensis*).

Lily-of-the-valley (*Convallaria majalis*).

Giant Cactus (*Cereus giganteus*).

Chrysanthemum frutescens.

Camomile (*Anthemis nobilis*).

Flower of the Giant Cactus (*Cereus giganteus*).

Cineraria of the Gardens (*Senecio cruentus*).

Mountain-tobacco (*Arnica montana*).

Camellia (*C. Japonica*).

A variety of *Gloxinia*.

Cypripedium Veitchii.

Arnotto (*Bixa Orellana*).

Dry Goods.

Express.

Farmer.

Fish-dealer.

Florist.

Flour and Feed.

Fruit.

Furniture.

Gent's Furnishing.

Glover.

Grocer.

Gunsmith.

Hair-dresser. (Ladies')

Hardware.

Harness-dealer.

Hatter.

Horseshoer.

Hosiery.

Ice.

Jeweler.

Lager-Beer.

Lamps and Oil.

Leather-dealer.

Liquor-dealer.

Lock-s'th & Bell-hanger.

Locomotive.

Lumber-dealer.

Machinist.

Marble-cutter.   Mason.   Masonic.   Milinery.

Mineral Waters.   Musical Instruments.   Music-store.   Naval.

Optician.   Oyster-house.   Painter. (House)   Piano-dealer.

Patriotic.   Pawnbroker.   Perfumery.   Restaurant.

Pickles & Preserves.   Picture-Frames.   Plumber.   Sewing-Machines.

Race. (Boat)   Race. (Horse)   Race. (Yacht)   Railroad. (Freight)

Sashes. Blinds & Doors.   Scale-maker.   Schooner.   Segar-dealer.

Shell-fish Dealer.

Ship-builder.

Ship-chandler.

Ship. (Clipper)

Shoe-makers' Findings.

Silver-ware.

Sloop.

Soap and Candles.

Stationer.

Steam-boat.

Steam-engine.

Steam-ship.

Stoves.

Surgical Instruments.

Tailor.

Tea-dealer.

Tin-ware.

Tobacconist.

Toy-dealer.

Trunks.

Undertaker.

Upholsterer.

Watches & Clocks.

Wheelwright.

Wine-dealer.

Willow-ware.

Wire-worker.

Wooden-ware.

Dress-maker.

Umbrella-dealer.

Military Goods.

Hair-dresser. (Gent's)

Fishing-tackle.

Livery-Stable.

Odd-Fellows.

Horse-dealer.

Furrier.

Yankee Notions.

Paper-hanger.

Kitchen-furnishing.

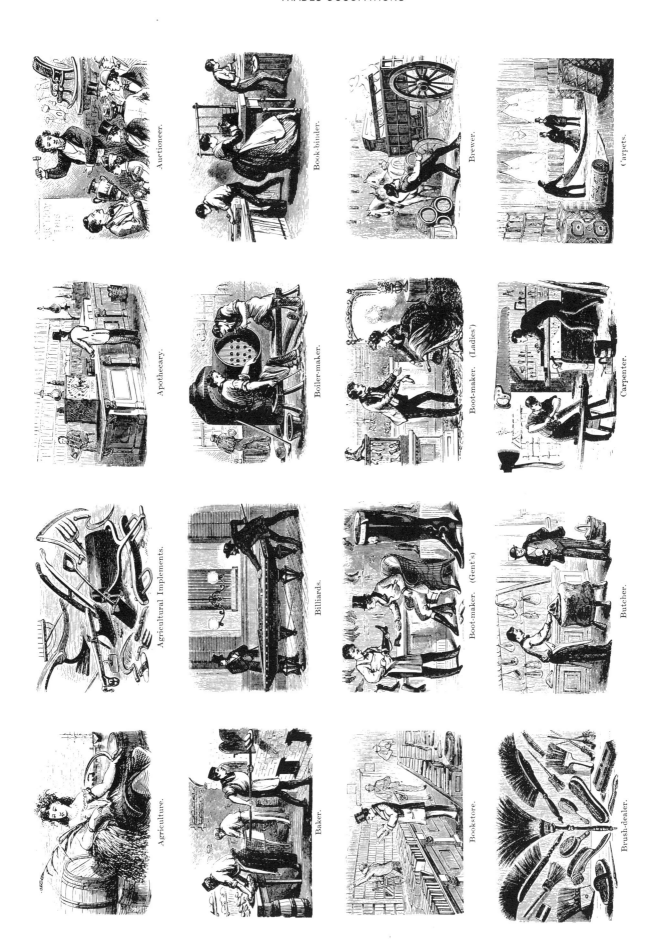

Plumber.

Sashes, Blinds and Doors.

Planter. (Tobacco)

Saddlery.

Sugar-mill at work

Planter. (Sugar)

Restaurant.

Sewing-Machine.

Planter. (Cotton)

Railroad. (Freight)

Segar-dealer.

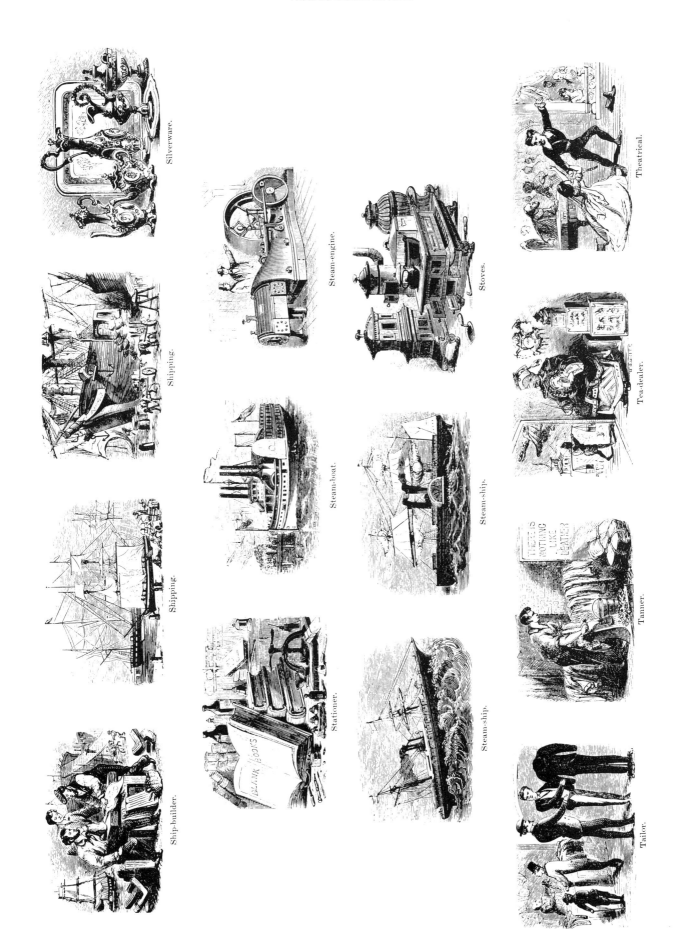

Silverware.

Steam-engine.

Stores.

Theatrical.

Shipping.

Steam-boat.

Steam-ship.

Tea-dealer.

Shipping.

Stationer.

Steam-ship.

Tanner.

Ship-builder.

Tailor.

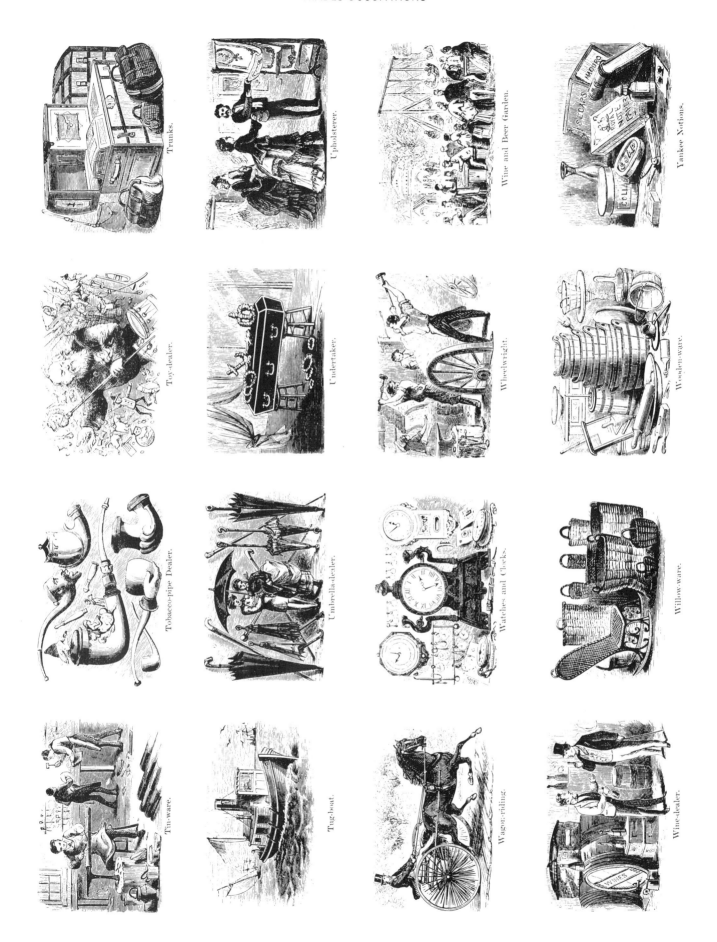

Trunks.

Upholsterer.

Wine and Beer Garden.

Yankee Notions.

Toy-dealer.

Undertaker.

Wheelwright.

Wooden-ware.

Tobacco-pipe Dealer.

Umbrella-dealer.

Watches and Clocks.

Willow-ware.

Tin-ware.

Tug-boat.

Wagon-riding.

Wine-dealer.

Mining-Cradle.

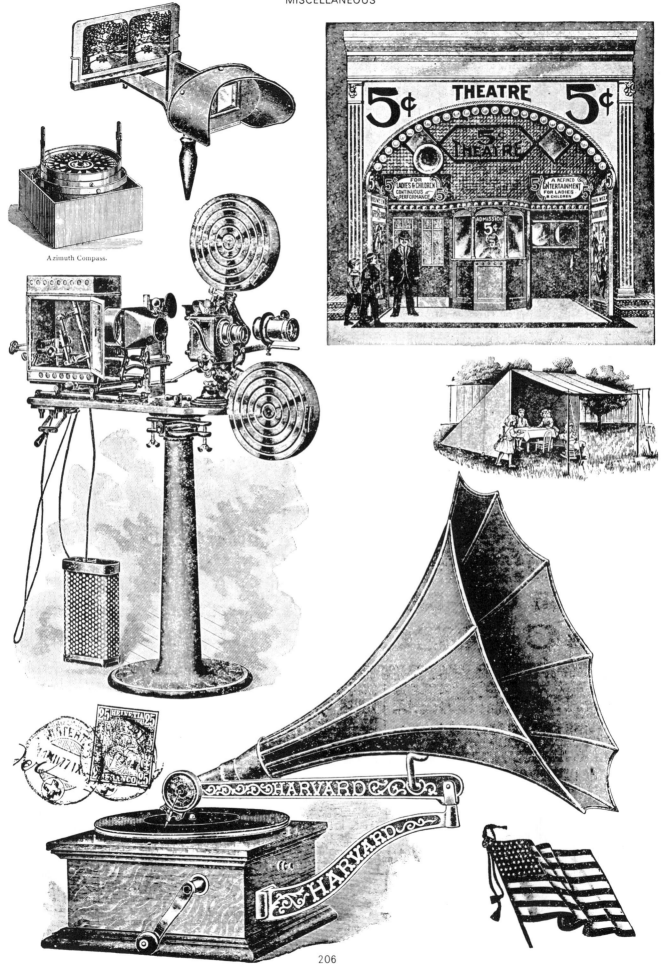

Azimuth Compass.

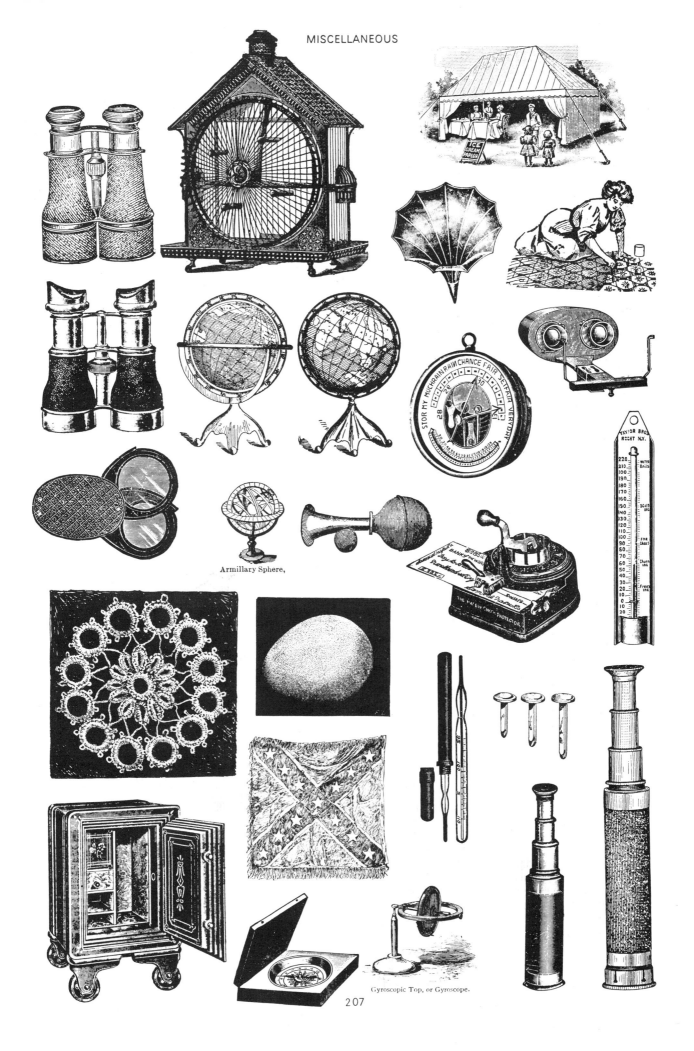

Armillary Sphere,

Gyroscopic Top, or Gyroscope.